Dear Mom

Women's
letters
of love,
loss, and
longing

*all best
wishes,*

*Deborah
Berger*

Edited by Deborah Berger

Printed in Victoria, Canada

Published by Trafford: January 2002

National Library of Canada
Cataloguing in Publication Data

Main entry under title:
  Dear Mom : women's letters of love, loss, and longing
  ISBN 1-55212-956-X
  I. Berger, Deborah, 1949- II. Mothers and daughters.
HQ755.86.D42 2001   306.874'3   C2001-903109-2

TRAFFORD

This book was published *on-demand* in cooperation with Trafford Publishing.
On-demand publishing is a unique process and service of making a book available for retail sale to the public taking advantage of on-demand manufacturing and Internet marketing. **On-demand publishing** includes promotions, retail sales, manufacturing, order fulfilment, accounting and collecting royalties on behalf of the author.

Suite 6E, 2333 Government St., Victoria, B.C. V8T 4P4, CANADA

Phone	250-383-6864	Toll-free	1-888-232-4444 (Canada & US)
Fax	250-383-6804	E-mail	sales@trafford.com
Web site	www.trafford.com	TRAFFORD PUBLISHING IS A DIVISION OF TRAFFORD HOLDINGS LTD.
Trafford Catalogue #01-0358		www.trafford.com/robots/01-0358.html

10   9   8   7   6   5   4

CONTENTS

Letters of Loss

Letters of Longing

Dear Reader

• • •

Dear Reader,

Every woman has stories to tell about her mother.

The mother she has, the mother she wants, the mother she misses, the mother she didn't know.

We carry our mothers with us. Sometimes we carry her in our hearts, in our heads—or on our backs. Sometimes we are connected to our mothers with the thick, strong cords of intertwined love and true acceptance; other times the bonds are stretched thin and taut, scratching against our consciousness, rubbing raw the sore spots in our souls.

But we are always linked to our mothers: both to the dreams of the mothers we wish for and the realities of the mothers we have. Even if our mother has been gone for years—for decades—the relationship is still very much alive. Mom is still with us: offering advice, encouragement, criticism, appreciation, rejection, solace. What we daughters do with this ongoing commentary— whether we unknowingly incorporate it into our reality, or consciously and carefully review it, deciding what to keep and what to put away—is fundamental to how fully we lead our own lives.

When I first started this project, I asked contributors to write letters about what they had never told their mothers. For whatever reason: because they had never found the words, because they had run out of time, because they were protecting their mothers, or because, simply and fundamentally, it was too great a risk to share such hidden thoughts and feelings.

In *Dear Mom*, you meet women who have stripped away pretenses, societal constraints, and basic fears to uncover and express their most private truths about their relationship with their mothers. You get to peer over the shoulders of the women, share in their laughter, and experience their struggles. You see how other women cast light on this most complicated, rewarding, and sometimes frustrating relationship. You witness women at different stages of their lives reflecting on the legacies their mothers (knowingly or unconsciously, but always powerfully) left them. You learn how other women experience the glories and the scars, the hurt and the healing that make up this most primal of connections.

You can almost hear the pens scratching and the keyboards clicking as women write to their mothers, living and dead, with the freedom of knowing the letter won't be mailed. (And in "Writing Your Own *Dear Mom* Letter," at the end of this book, I invite you to do the same, and offer some suggestions to help you get started.) Because I wanted contributors to be able to express their most private truths, they had the option of not using their real names in this book—a choice made by eight of the 25 contributors.

You also get to meet the women behind the letters, since each *Dear Mom* letter is followed by a profile of the contributor. You learn about the surprises, satisfactions, and challenges they faced in writing down their most private truths.

The 25 *Dear Mom* contributors include women from a variety of backgrounds, careers, religions, and lifestyles. They include (present and former) teachers, business owners, homemakers, real estate agents, artists, secretaries, social workers, journalists, and government officials. Some are accomplished professionals, well-known in their fields and public figures in their communities. They are married, single, divorced, widowed. Many, though not all, are mothers themselves.

Many contributors are baby boomers, in their 40s and 50s. Others are in their 60s, 70s, and 80s. (The oldest contributor is over 90; her conversation with her mother continues!)

Think of these letters as snapshots; they represent the writer's truth *at the time* the letter was written. I worked on this book for three years; the factual information (specific jobs, ages, etc.) is accurate *as of the time* each letter and profile were written and initially edited. Since then, of course, we have all gotten a little older, but, as one of my contributors happily pointed out, not in these pages.

Each contributor reviewed edited versions of her letter and of her profile. I conducted the interviews and wrote the profiles. In editing the letters, I wanted to preserve the writer's voice and her vision. Often I questioned the contributor about the details of her letter, and these clarifications were included in subsequent versions of her letter and biography. The final edits of both the letters and the profiles were my responsibility.

As the letters came in, I began to see a pattern: of love, loss, and longing. Of course life is much more complicated than can be summed up in a single word, and some of the letters could easily be placed in all three categories, others in two. My difficulty in deciding where to put many letters testifies to the complexity of our lives and our truths.

I hope that reading these letters, and meeting the courageous women who wrote them, will offer warmth and hope as you move along the winding path of understanding your relationship with your own mother.

• • •

Note: *When a full first and last name is given in the letter and the profile, the contributor is using her real name. When only a first name is used, that name and identifying details have been changed to protect privacy.*

Dear Mom

Women's
letters
of love

Carolyn Wynhausen Sperry

remembers her mother's strength and fierce independence—staunch allies during a battle with cancer.

• • •

Dear Mom,

You used to ask me, "Am I a good mother?" You didn't ask this question often. But often enough to suggest your anxiety. Now, when I look back as an adult, in style and comportment you never seemed an anxious person. To me, especially when I was little and you were young beyond imagination, far younger than I am now, you always seemed elegant and strong: the epitome of ability, wisdom, and caring. My true north. You had the location, the instinct, the sense.

So my answer to your question was always, "Yes." "Yes."

Yes, you were a good mother. But—and I did not add this "but," as you knew it better than I—you were very flawed. You had a rotten, Irish temper that could scorch whole harvests. You drank too much. You bellyached about your family whom you deeply loved. And about your in-laws whom you tried to love—even occasionally succeeding. Too often, you turned getting ready for their visits, whether for dinner or an extended stay, into a civil defense action. As all mothers do to all children, you embarrassed me.

But it seems now as if none of the embarrassment much matters. You were one hell of a woman. Fierce, indignant, brave beyond speech. You took no prisoners. Yet you accepted people, including their failures and peccadilloes. And you loved a good time. You told wonderful stories. You loved to laugh. Yet you could be so tender and vulnerable.

When Dad had his breakdown, and I was too young to understand—or care—you held us all together. You confronted Oma and Opa. You insisted they realize that their adored son was imploding into a complete collapse. You made our lives seem normal when Dad spent six months having shock treatments at the hospital, and wasn't well enough to work for another six when he finally could come home. I remember that Christmas, how I sat in the living room, smitten by our little tree. I thought it was the most beautiful Christmas tree in the world. You had trimmed it with nothing but tiny hand-tied red ribbons. Decades later, when I recalled that tiny tree adorned with shimmering red bows, you said ribbon was all you could afford that year.

As I write this letter, I feel such a deep childhood sense of your presence, your power, your physical resplendence. You adored clothes. I remember you and Auntie and the long ride to the endless millinery. The feathers, buttons, ribbons. The textures and fabric. The fragrances. All the female exotica of what was probably a small, modest shop owned by another woman trying to eke out a living after World War II. Yet in my childhood memory, I had entered with my mother and my adored great aunt into an inner sanctum of female desire and sensibility. You knew how to make things. You had studied design in New York before you married Dad. You had to make things. And if you had to make them, you would make them stylish.

More than 20 years ago, I began the first fragments of a still-unfinished poem for you. I called it "Litany for My Mother's Body." By then I was a mother several times myself and I came to this impulse of praise and lamentation as I watched your beautiful, tall, elegant body become increasingly eroded, disfigured by age, illness, arthritis. That was before the cancer.

You called. You said you had "the big C." You said the tumors felt like a string with little knots tied in it. I remember exactly where I was when you told me this. You endured, more than chose, a mastectomy. Months later you showed me your prosthesis. Years later, you said you'd rather die than have another mastectomy. You said you felt mutilated.

Eighteen years after the mastectomy, the doctors diagnosed bone cancer. You said you weren't afraid to die. You weren't, but you still had lots more life in you, more life to keep loving the people you loved. You wanted to see your grandchildren unfold. You kept outdistancing medical expectations. And not simply because you got expert care and treatment. That mattered. But Annie and I think it was really because you *skipped* so many of your chemo appointments. Your oncologist once told me you were "fiercely independent;" he said you'd canceled at least half your appointments. I laughed out loud. He didn't know a quarter of it. I told him you skipped the treatments because they made you feel like a whipped dog. He said, on the contrary, that "you tolerated them very well." I knew both claims were true. They just spoke to different realities. You liked your food and drink, and the chemo laid you out for two days after.

You didn't tell us how much you suffered. You bitched about other things. About cancer you didn't much complain. Once you said you felt sorrier about it for Dad than for yourself. Once, perhaps six months before you died, we visited while you lay in bed. You'd doze a bit, then you'd wake, and we'd visit some again. All at once, you turned to me and cried out, as if distraught by a poor performance, "Oh, it's taking me so long to die."

But I see now how stupid we were, how the painkillers didn't do enough to kill your pain, and how we were so stupid—we didn't realize we could have done more. When we'd talk by phone, I'd ask, "Mom, how are you feeling?" You'd answer, "I'm still breathing." And the inflection in your voice made that answer funny and loving and true at the same time. And then we'd talk about something else. I didn't comprehend how much you spared us.

Growing up, I loved to sit and visit with you while you primped in your dressing room. Two months before dying, you told me you hated to look at what had now become your scrawny body in the mirror. Right then I should have cried out, "Look in our hearts instead, Mom!"

Dad said, "The longer I knew her, the better I liked her."

And your question? Were you a good mother?

The real answer is, "No."

Good is too paltry a word for the human being you kept becoming. You were fierce, and difficult. Smart, funny, and loving. No, you weren't a good mother. You were a *magnificent* one.

• • •

PROFILE: Carolyn (a.k.a. Winnie) Sperry

For most of Carolyn Sperry's life, friends and colleagues have known her as "Winnie," a compression of her maiden name of Wynhausen. But her mother heartily disliked the nickname and most definitely preferred the name she picked out for her daughter. In tribute to her mother, Carolyn is using her given name in this book.

It's an understatement to say that Carolyn has a busy, rather complicated life. So it takes awhile for us to find a time to do her interview. As we walk toward a restaurant in her urban neighborhood, a bustling community with almost the feel of a small town, we meet someone she knows on every block. Carolyn has just driven back from a business trip, but she is still energetic and focused.

Tell me about your work and your family.

I'm 57 (ouch!) years old. I have four children: three fully adult and one 18 year old. I've been married 32 years.

I would say, definitely, that I've always tried to build my work around the responsibilities, pleasures, and blessings of raising children, and of being married to a wonderful man. Family has always taken precedence in my decision making.

I've managed to do a variety of things. I was an adjunct professor of sociology for 14 years at a nearby university. I started Mother Sperry's Plum Pudding—a small, seasonal, specialty-food business—20 years ago, and it's alive and well. I've been a board member of an amazing nonprofit community clinic for 15 years, and I am active in my church community.

In the 1980s, I ran a small, Sunday breakfast parlor and made it a family operation. My oldest daughter, Katherine, still calls it "the breakfast parlor from hell"! I've tried to do useful or interesting work, preferably both. It's been fun.

Why did you decide to write a Dear Mom letter?

I thought the idea was a stroke of genius. Really. If there is a deeper primal bond than that between mother and child, I don't know of it.

And I was crazy about my mother—even though she sometimes made me crazy!

My mother died six years ago of cancer, yet she's quite alive in me. Writing the letter gave me a chance to honor her triumph over fear and pain and, as it developed, to point out my own family's failure to realize that we could have—if we'd known—done even more than we did to help her avoid unnecessary suffering. I wanted to send up a flag about that for women who read the letter.

Were there any surprises for you when you were writing your Dear Mom letter?

I've thought a lot about my mother and I think I knew mostly what I wanted to say to her. *(She pauses.)* But I was writing the letter from the vantage point now of a middle-aged woman. And one surprise was realizing—*recognizing*—just how young, inexperienced, and vulnerable my mother was when my father became ill and had to be hospitalized.

She was only about 30 then. She had two young children: I was 4, and my brother was 7. (My younger brother and sister arrived later.) Mom must have been remarkably strong: She kept things normal for us; we had no sense of insecurity.

Dad was very ill. He'd had a complete emotional collapse; it was the late 1940s and psychiatric hospitals used shock treatment. No one knew if Dad would recover. As I was writing my letter, I was struck by the burden my mother must have had.

Of course at the time I was so little I didn't know any of this. It was only later, when I was a teenager, that my mother actually told me much of what had happened. At that time, I could sense some of what she must have gone through—the anxiety, fear, and not knowing what was going to happen. But now, at my age, I can see how strong she was.

When Mom went to the hospital to visit Dad, my brother and I usually stayed with family or friends. Except one time. I remember vividly how long the drive to the hospital seemed. When we got there, we were not allowed to see my father. A male nurse was put in charge of us. He was darling and got into entertaining us with his very fancy harmonica with buttons on it. I was so entranced I didn't even think about my father. Besides, I didn't know what a hospital was. I only knew I didn't want to leave when Mom came back, because I was enjoying myself so much.

Dad had to stay in the hospital for six months. Various family members helped Mom out with finances. My father had been starting up a small business when he became ill. His business partner walked out on him. My father understood this; he said the man had a family to support. But my mother never forgave this man who came back after Dad was well and the business was more stable. Dad, on the other hand, said, "Hey, he was a good engineer." As a courtesy to Dad, Mom would, under protest, agree to let this partner come to the house, but she would not let him sit at her table, and she would have disemboweled herself rather than feed him dinner.

How would you describe yourself now?

Very lucky. I've had many privileges and blessings in my life. I grew up in a stable family, with tremendous loyalty and a sense of support. Yes, there were plenty of times when we didn't agree, but in our family you accepted differences among family members; it didn't affect the sense of commitment you felt toward people you loved and who loved you. There was this incredible solidarity. I think my husband and I have passed that on to our children.

I am a very secure person. Even when I didn't do what I was supposed to, my parents were there. My mother gave me a great sense of self. She raised me to believe in my own mind.

Has your mother influenced you in the way you are a mother?

(She pauses, thinks about this.) Yes. One of the things my mother tried to encourage was a sense of autonomy, independence, and responsibility. You could make mistakes, but you needed to be responsible. You were entitled to bungle things, as long as you took responsibility for your failures, which also meant you learned to take credit for your successes. Mom was a good booster, very positive and supportive, but not obnoxiously overt. She taught me to distinguish between a specific action, its outcome, and who I was.

The fundamental message was, "Go ahead and make mistakes. That's how you learn. You're not going to lose our love." I think that was a great lesson.

I followed her example, encouraging my children to be responsible for their own choices, because that's so much a part of who you are. I thought my mother was a wonderful role model in that way.

Both my parents were very generous in their acceptance of people. They took people's eccentricities, peccadilloes and failures along with their virtues. I can still remember one of the very few times I ever heard my father say a critical word about anyone!

Mom, however, was more plainspoken about people's shortcomings, but she didn't cast people out. We had some relatives who were racist. My mother hated that, she argued with them, but she never ostracized them. She loved them even though some of their attitudes made her indignant. It showed me you can love people deeply and disavow some of their values and beliefs.

What do you consider to be your biggest successes and accomplishments?

No doubt, raising kids. (And please note, I'm a feminist.) And getting to have loving and trusting, albeit sometimes challenging, relationships with my now adult children. That's absolutely number one.

Having also a wonderful, if not always easy, relationship with my husband. *(She laughs.)* After that, the rest is gravy.

It's been good gravy. I've been able to do interesting and useful work. Paid and unpaid. I'm committed to being an active member of a larger world. I believe in working for social justice. My friend, Hazel Wolf, a hero, used to say: "You do what you can. Then you do some more." Hazel had it exactly right.

And of course, and this is not insignificant: the benefits and pleasures of many wonderful friends. I am absolutely a people person.

Your biggest disappointments or regrets?

I have to think about this.

I can't really think of any.

Maybe tonight or tomorrow I'll come up with something.

Let me put it this way: No major regrets. I have a lot of small disappointments, although right at this moment I'd be hard pressed to name a single one.

(Having thought about it, Carolyn later followed up with two disappointments.)

One is not having realized that there was even more we could have done to alleviate Mom's suffering from bone cancer.

Another is having lost a dear and special friend from an estrangement many years ago.

Angela B. Ginorio

left home in part to break free from her protective mother. Now in midlife, Angela treasures their close connection across the miles.

• • •

Querida mami (Dear Mom),

I'm in a writing mood, the way I get after three days of sun when I've had some time off. We're all doing well, Emi is growing by the day (vertically), and we're trying not to grow horizontally.

I have something important to share with you—something that has been triggered by the recent death of my friend Ana Mari's mom.

When I left home at 24, eager to be different from you, not to repeat your life, one of my goals was to not need you anymore. At that time, I was putting physical distance between us, so that I could develop the psychological distance necessary to be "myself."

Today, 29 years later and more than 3,500 miles from you, I find "myself" in a very different position. The miles that separate us dissolve every time we talk to each other on the phone. Almost all the time, I'm the one initiating the phone call; it's a ritual that acknowledges I have greater resources, but more than that, it's a demonstration of my love for you.

As you have passed your eightieth year and I have passed my fiftieth, the time we spend together becomes more precious. Death has always been a reality in our lives, but the deaths of two of your brothers last year and of a friend's mother this month have foreshadowed that possibility. Either one of us could die, but *por ley de vida* (by the law of life), it is more likely to be you.

In a reversal of that flight of 24 years ago when I wanted to put distance between us, today I face the possibility of your death with terror. One of the places where that terror comes from is the realization that you are the last direct link not only to my youth but also to the Puerto Rico of my past. Like all immigrants, I want my daughter to love that land too. You're an integral part of that landscape for her as well as for me.

So I write you this letter, asking you not to die. Don't even think about it! Add a new petition to your daily prayers: "Oh God, let me live until my daughter does not need me anymore." (I know what you're thinking: "God knows what is best, He'll know when that is." Okay, if you have to say it that way; you know Him better than I do.)

Give my love to *titi* (Auntie) Betty and the rest of the family. Talk to you next Saturday.

Un abrazo bien fuerte, de tu hija (A big hug from your daughter).

PROFILE: Angela B. Ginorio

Angela Ginorio meets me for lunch in a neighborhood restaurant. She has thick, dark hair, an entrancing voice, and an energetic, enthusiastic manner.

Tell me about your work and your family.

Let's see. I'm 53. I'm an associate professor in the Women's Studies Department at the University of Washington. I got my Ph.D. in social psychology from Fordham University in New York.

I grew up in Puerto Rico, the oldest of three children. I was the only girl. My mother stayed home and took care of the family. We lived in the country, about 15 minutes or so from the University of Puerto Rico. But it was rural, not suburban.

My father was 20 years older than my mom. He worked for a dairy company. He bought the delivery trucks and he oversaw the maintenance of the vehicles.

My parents were very religious Catholics. I went to the nearest parochial Catholic school, from second grade through high school. Both my parents had finished only the eighth grade. They wanted their children to go to college.

I got my bachelor's and a master's in psychology from the University of Puerto Rico. During this time, I had a boyfriend; he was a student leader, from a wealthy, well-known family. My father didn't like my boyfriend. They had different politics. My boyfriend came from a very conservative, Republican family. My father was a social democrat, a leftist, and a supporter of independence for Puerto Rico.

Still, my family was very traditional: The whole five years I was with my boyfriend, I lived at home, and we saw each other at the University. He came to my house just three times, and we never actually had a date! If I went out with my girlfriends, my 15-year-old brother went along as a chaperone. *(I show my ignorance of this tradition by being amazed.)* Yes, it's true! A proper young woman did not go out at night by herself, or just with her girlfriends.

After I got my master's, I was working as an acting assistant professor at the University of Puerto Rico, but I knew I needed to get my Ph.D. At the time, the University did not have a Ph.D. program in psychology.

When I was 23, my boyfriend broke my heart and split up with me after five years. My mentor in the psychology department was happy about this; I was stunned at his reaction. He suggested that I apply to Harvard, Princeton, George Washington, and Fordham. Fordham gave me the most money, so I went to Fordham. I had been to New York City just once before.

Living in New York City was a big adjustment. My parish priest knew a priest at Fordham, and he found me a place to stay with a nun for the first 10 days. I had never met a nun like her. This was 1971, and she was a nun who didn't wear a habit—and she smoked! She was getting her Ph.D. in sociology at Fordham.

After a few days, I got a roommate and an apartment. Eventually, I had a boyfriend. Mom had told me, "Don't let a boyfriend in the apartment. He will try to kiss you." So I let my boyfriend in my apartment to use the bathroom—but no kiss! This "no kissing" didn't last. *(We both laugh.)*

I left Fordham in 1976. In my academic career I've worked at different places. I spent two years at the University of Illinois at Champaign-Urbana. My father became very ill when I was there. For almost three months, while he was sick, I would spend two weeks in Illinois, and then two weeks in Puerto Rico. The professor who was my supervisor was great about it. My father died when he was 74, of lung cancer.

When I was an acting assistant professor in psychology at Bowling Green University, I met Chip, the man I later married. My mother had just about given up on me, I was so "old"—at 33! I called my mother and told her I was serious about the guy.

I told her he was divorced, and she said, "Any children?"

"No."

"Is he Catholic?"

"No, Mom, he's Episcopalian."

She said, "Close enough!"

Chip and I dated for four years. Now we've been married 16 years, and we have a 12-year-old daughter, Emi.

Why did you decide to write a **Dear Mom** *letter?*

When I left Puerto Rico, I wanted to get away from my mother. I owe her my life. Not just my physical life, but my philosophy. My mother is a wonderful person. Over the years, we have communicated at least weekly: first by letters, now by phone. I have a very rich life, but there are still so many conversations I haven't had with her.

Were there any surprises for you when you were writing your **Dear Mom** *letter?*

In some ways, I was surprised by what I chose to write. When I was first asked, I thought my letter would be about the generational ties between my mother, myself, and my daughter Emi. But it ended up being about this intense need of mine.

How would you describe yourself now?

I would say, the mother of a 12 year old. And I'm in a moment of transition. For the first time in 17 years, I'm not an administrator, so I can choose more what I want to do.

And death is very present right now. A friend's mother just died, and I have four friends who have cancer. My mother came to visit me, and I could see she's aging. We're all aging.

Has your mother influenced you in the way you are a mother?

Oh yes. *(With emphasis.)*

Both in the ways I do things and in how I don't do things.

My mother loved us without any reservations. Even when she was angry, we knew she loved us. It was clear, there was no doubt, we always knew. I do that with my daughter, too.

My mother did not shield me from the bad things in life—somebody dying or being sick. I do the same with my daughter.

In terms of what not to do, my mother would lose her temper really easily. I *try* not to do that. *(She laughs.)*

My mother insisted that we eat the food on our plates. This I was determined I would not do. I didn't want a power struggle about food. Whatever my daughter wants, she eats. It's interesting, because she does eat well-balanced meals.

What do you consider to be your biggest successes and accomplishments?
My daughter. My network of friends.

Your biggest disappointments or regrets?
(She pauses, thinks about this question.) I would be a sociologist or anthropologist instead of a social psychologist, because I think the focus on the individual in psychology is misguided.

I would not have let my eleventh-grade chemistry teacher dissuade me from science.

I regret not being a poet. *(She smiles.)*

Really, there are very few things I would do differently.

Teresa Wippel

reflects on the career choices her mother, like so many women of that generation, never got to make.

• • •

Dear Mom,

Like so many mothers today, I sometimes struggle to make my way through this uncharted territory known as "combining motherhood with career." During that emotional tug of war between guilt that I'm not doing enough and confidence that I've raised the best kids on the planet, I can't help but make comparisons between your life and mine.

You "stayed at home," because in your generation, there were few women who did otherwise. Of course, Heidi, my friend in early elementary school, had a mother who worked. She came home from school to an empty house and had to call her mom at work every day, to let her know she had arrived. Heidi didn't have a very happy childhood. Her mother was strict and unfriendly, and at the time I was sure it was because she worked. I remember being horrified when you suggested, jokingly, that you should get a job. "Do you want me to be like Heidi?" I whined.

Yet I also remember so clearly a moment years later, after I had finished college and was working as a newspaper journalist. You said, "I think that would have been the career I would have chosen." And it struck me that no one had really given you that choice. You were a waitress and a secretary out of necessity to support your family when you were a young widow. But once you met and married my father, you were content to leave the 9-to-5 routine for a blended family of six children, and to start anew with a baby (me) a year later.

You would have been a marvelous journalist. I can't remember a time during my childhood when you didn't have a newspaper spread out on the table. You watched the television news at noon, dinnertime, and 11 o'clock. You have always been a voracious reader and a lover of words. I remember the games of Scrabble we played and how crossword puzzles were your constant companion.

Now, at 75, you still can't stand to miss a television news show or the morning paper. Books and crossword puzzles cover your coffee table. You are a news junkie— and proud of it.

It's clear that I have you to thank for my love of the written word. Writing and editing are my greatest strengths, and even though I am no longer a newspaper reporter, I still can't miss my morning paper.

I'm proud to tell you that your grandchildren, 7 and 11, are the spelling champions of their class. Your grandson spots typographical errors in school textbooks. And the three of us play Scrabble together regularly.

You take great pride in your role as a mother, and there truly is no more important job than successful parenting. I will never be able to tell you how much I appreciate the love, support, and friendship you have given me throughout my life. But I wish that you could have also realized the joy of being a published writer. I'm certain you would have discovered, as I have, that writing feeds the mind and nourishes the soul.

Members of my generation are breaking new ground when it comes to expectations about being a mother and maintaining a career. But we couldn't have done it without moms like you encouraging us along the way. You never put any limits on what my future could be, and that is the greatest gift you could have given me.

Walking down this new path isn't always easy, and the travel plan is slightly different for every woman I know. I'm certain that it will be easier for your granddaughter and future generations to find that balance between working and family. Everyone deserves a chance to follow her dreams, and no one should be left wondering what could have been.

• • •

PROFILE: Teresa Wippel

Teresa Wippel, tall, slender and blonde, comes to the interview in a bit of a rush. She's an extremely busy senior editorial producer at Go2Net, an Internet company that was growing exponentially at the time. We order our food at a downtown café and sit. She focuses intently on my questions.

From the way she frames her answers, it's obvious she has thought a lot about many of these topics.

Tell me about your work and your family.
I'm 42. I've been married 17 years. I have two children.

Why did you decide to write a **Dear Mom** *letter?*
Over all these years, I've always been close to my mom, but there are things I've never actually said. I don't see her that often. She lives in Arizona, a couple of thousand miles away. I think about her getting older. I wanted to memorialize the relationship, to put it in writing and know it would be published.

Were there any surprises for you when you were writing your **Dear Mom** *letter?*
Yes. When I reread the letter after setting it aside for a few months, I was surprised at how much meaning it held for me. I had been thinking about these things for years, and I didn't realize how therapeutic it would be for me to put my thoughts down on paper. I remember so clearly when my mom said she would have been a journalist: That really stuck with me. When I was writing my letter, I was focusing on my feelings and my appreciation of my mother and her unrealized talents. I want my daughter to have the opportunities I've had—and more.

I could see, from looking at my mom's life and mine, how far women have come.

How would you describe yourself now?

I'm really happy with how I've turned out.

My life is very full and rich. I feel really fortunate to have a wonderful family and good personal and professional relationships that I enjoy. I have a supportive husband. My kids are great. Now that they're getting older, I can do things as friends with them. Where I am now, I wouldn't change anything.

In terms of professional accomplishment, I'm proud of what I've done. I know people respect my work and know I'm reliable, dependable, and treat people fairly.

I value more and more my long-term friendships. They make life more interesting. You need friends and with such a busy life, sometimes they come last—which is unfortunate. Yet I still feel conflicted about the family-job pull. I haven't met a woman in my age group who doesn't feel this way. We still have this need to be in charge of everything.

Most of the time, I'm okay with the balancing act. The struggle comes from the expectations we put on ourselves. This past weekend, I was going to make a cake for my family, for Valentine's Day, because I'll be at a meeting that night and won't be home. I didn't have time to do it. I was rushing around with the kids' sports and all the rest.

Sometimes, I still run into a woman who says, "You work full-time! Are your kids okay?" That comes back to my letter. Whenever I wonder whether I should work, I think about my mom. I don't want to be saying to my children, I wish I would have done this or that. Where I work, a lot of the other women are younger than me. I hear them talk about their mothers, who didn't work outside the home and now are in their 50s. When their kids leave, the women experience this tremendous hole, because they don't have something that's their own.

Has your mother influenced you in the way you are a mother?

Yes. *(With emphasis.)*

The overall feeling I had growing up was of warmth and affection, to live life and enjoy it, not get caught up in worrisome details. Mom had rules, but she wasn't overly strict. I remember it made me feel she trusted me. I want to give my kids that sense too. My mom was really easygoing: She was not a nitpicky housekeeper, and I'm like that, too. But she also thought school and homework were very important, and I'm like that, a real stickler about those things.

The other way she influenced me was about money. She was pretty frugal. She has a sense of price. I have a tendency to be that way—I'm trying to teach my kids to compare prices, to be conscious about how they spend money.

What do you consider to be your biggest successes and accomplishments?

Probably my biggest accomplishment is the kind of kids my husband and I have raised. We get compliments from teachers and other parents, just about how nice and thoughtful they are. It helps us realize we've done a good job. None of my professional accomplishments measures up to raising two really good human beings who help others, who are positive leaders. Nobody else can do that except my husband and me.

Your biggest disappointments or regrets?

You know, I guess it would be the road not taken. What would have happened if I had followed my original path—to be a press secretary for a congressman? Or I could have become CEO of a company.

I guess I'll always wonder what I missed by not following those roads. I know I have the talent to do those things. But I don't necessarily regret my decisions. I couldn't have done them and also had enough time for my family.

Barbara Eisner

holds dear her mother's loving "life lessons" and passes them on to her children.

• • •

Dear Mom,

Though your body left this earth more than 18 years ago, you are still with me every day.

I know that to you, family love was the most important bond. Were you especially careful to make all of your children feel loved because you had been a child without a mother or father?

I think now about how it must have felt for you to be an orphan, coming from Russia to be raised by your brother Zolman and his wife, Bessie. I know they loved you, and you loved them, but I'm sure a great deal was missing. I remember your telling me in 1961, when you were so ill, how you still wished for your mother.

Now, I write this letter and I look at pictures of you. I wonder, who was Florence Okner? As a young woman, the photographs show you were an attractive woman, somewhat stylish in your dress. You liked jazz music. That was the life you had before I knew you. I guess children—even adult children—think of their parents' lives only in relationship to their own.

LOVE

You told us about the wonderful wedding Bessie and Zolman made for you and Dad, despite tight money. Mom, I still have your wedding dress, wrapped carefully, in my closet. The lace is in perfect condition.

I often think about the story of my birth as you told it one afternoon when you, Sandra, and I attended a luncheon together. I was born on a Saturday, so Dad was at the market in Perth Amboy. There was no telephone, so he didn't know that his second daughter had been born. When Dad came home, old Mr. Shecter was sitting on the front porch of the six-family house where we lived. He greeted Dad with a flap of the hand and a condescending, "It's another girl." Your closing remark to the telling of this story was, "What did he know?"— said with a flap of your hand to denote your disdain for this comment. I love this story, because it helps me remember how happy you were that day, sharing a good time with your daughters.

When you were 49, you became seriously ill. You had major surgery: a total hysterectomy. As was customary in 1961, you were not told that you had ovarian cancer. I came home from college to be with you, but no one told me you had cancer. A few weeks later, Dad broke the news to me. The doctors were not encouraging, and Dad didn't seem hopeful. I was devastated. I think it was the end of my innocence, the first time I really had to face the possibility that you, my beloved mother, could die.

You were so weak after your surgery, and the radiation treatment sapped your energy even more. I had never seen you so frail.

Right about this time, Jerry and I became engaged. Was it right to make wedding plans with my mother so ill? I was filled with conflicted feelings, including—I must confess with a bit of shame—some resentment that this time, which should have been pure joy, was marred by your illness and an unknown prognosis.

But you got stronger each day. In July we had a big wedding with all the trimmings. I'm the only one of my friends with movies of her wedding. (No videos in those days.) I am so grateful you were there to see me married, and that you were doing well. Mom, our movie has been transferred to video, and I treasure it. When your nephew Roman visited from Russia, he was overwhelmed that he could see you, Bessie, and Zolman "alive."

Despite the bleak outcome predicted by your physicians, you lived 21 more years. Though the last three years of your life were clouded with illness caused by another cancer, I will always be grateful for the years that you had. Those were the years when I had children, and they had the privilege of knowing their grandmother.

You are still a part of their lives, as you are of mine. We often joke about my daughter Mindy's lack of neatness, a trait you tried to instill in her. You would go to my daughters' rooms and show them how easy it was to keep them neat. It didn't work then, Mom, and the situation hasn't changed much, even today. But my daughters and I still talk with the utmost affection about you and your "obsession" with cleaning. That is who you were, and we love you for it.

The kitchen was your domain. Your cooking wasn't fancy—but very flavorful. Just recently, Sandra met an old friend from high school who reminded her of the wonderful steaks you made by putting mustard on the meat before broiling it. I had forgotten about that. It was heartening to know that someone outside of the family carried around memories of you.

Your Chambers stove was a beautiful sight, with its shiny stainless steel top. It was a unique stove to purchase in 1950, and it is still prized today. Mom, we saw a version of your stove selling for $6,000 at an antique and collectible show in New York. What could yours have cost in 1950?

Sometimes when I would invite you and Dad for dinner, and then Sandy would invite you the same week, you would say, with such pride and affection, "I should have had more daughters. I wouldn't have to cook. I could eat at their houses every night of the week."

Mom, since you died, I have struggled with the concept of perpetuity. Do I believe in an afterlife? I'm not sure. I would like to think that you know about our lives now and that your spirit is there to help when adversity comes.

Mom, you taught me such valuable life lessons. You taught me to be careful what you say to other people, impressing upon me that once something is said, you can't take it back.

You cautioned me not to take sides if two people have a dispute. You said they would make up and forget what caused their argument, but always remember what I had said. What good advice. (I tried to pass it on to my own daughter just last week, but the present generation thinks that *truth* reigns supreme.) When we leave this earth, we are remembered for our deeds. And your life was filled with good deeds.

Your goodness was known to many. You taught me to treat people with respect and consideration. From you I learned the value of giving to charity and the importance of supporting Jewish causes. You bestowed life membership in Hadassah on Sandra and me, and I've done the same with my daughters.

My husband Jerry describes you as the purest person he has known. I've met people who say you were an angel. Your life was not an easy one, but maybe an easy life makes a person too complacent? Adversity helped you to strive for a better life for your children, and Mom, you succeeded in providing that.

My life is very different from the one you had. My first advantages were having parents alive, being born in the United States, and being able to enjoy a peaceful, uncomplicated childhood. I had the benefit of going to college and training for my profession as a pharmacist. I was a working mother well before it became the norm.

Yet in many ways, I am as old-fashioned as you were. My husband, children, and grandchildren are the most important people in my life. There is no professional success that could compete with the joy of my family. Though I have worked throughout my marriage, I always characterized it by saying I had a job, not a career. A career would have taken too much time from my family. I like having large crowds for holiday dinners. I want my home to be a place for my family to gather. My grandsons think this is their second home. They are a blessing. I've carried on your tradition of making poppy-seed cookies, and the children love them. Like you, I keep cookie dough in the freezer, so I can bake cookies on a whim.

At your funeral, the rabbi read from the liturgy, "A Woman of Valor." It describes a woman whose "price is above rubies." It is a poem that has been used to describe many women, but to me it was written for you, my dearest mother. I thank you for all your love and valuable life lessons.

• • •

PROFILE: Barbara Eisner

I meet Barbara Eisner in the lobby of the hotel where she is staying during a visit to Seattle. She looks very pulled together, attractive, and well dressed. We go across the street to have coffee and talk.

Tell me about your work and your family.

I'm 60. I've been married for 38 years. My husband owns an auto repair business. I have two adult daughters.

I've worked as a pharmacist virtually my entire married life, mostly part-time. I worked in a county long-term care facility for 25 years, and in a tuberculosis clinic. Now I'm semi-retired, and I only work one day a week in a clinic. I work with new patients, explaining how the medications work and how to take them.

When I was growing up, my parents encouraged higher education for their three children. I went to Temple University in Philadelphia. I had an interest in science, and I wanted a job I could do part-time and combine with a family. So pharmacy was a good fit for me.

Why did you decide to write a **Dear Mom** *letter?*

I thought it was a wonderful opportunity to express my feelings for my mother. Not a day goes by that I don't think of her. She's been gone 18 years, but her legacy lives on. She was an integral part of my life, and also of my daughters' lives as they were growing up.

Were there any surprises for you when you were writing your **Dear Mom** *letter?*

Yes. Some details were so clear. Some things in the past felt fresh, like they just happened. When I wrote about my mother, sister, and me attending a luncheon together, I could clearly picture the three of us together. I still can.

How would you describe yourself now?

I'm a wife, a mother, and a friend. I'm very satisfied with my life. Thankful and grateful. I love to be surrounded by my family and my friends.

I consider myself always having been an adult. If the child part of me ever existed, I left it behind. I don't remember ever being frivolous. I have always been someone people come to for advice. I'm a practical person.

Has your mother influenced you in the way you are a mother?

Yes. My children's needs came before my needs. That is like my mother: For her, the children came first. Nothing was too much for her. I feel the same way. If there's something I can do for my children, it's my pleasure. I'm someone they can depend on for moral support. There's mutual respect between my daughters and myself. I'm very close with them.

There were ways in which I was a different mother from my own. Mom had a lot of fears. I did not want to pass that along to my children. I encouraged my kids to be athletic, whereas my mother did not do that. She would watch us riding our bikes, afraid we would have an accident. But you know, there comes a time when you have to let go.

What do you consider to be your biggest successes and accomplishments?

A successful marriage, nice children, a close family, and a lot of friends.

My job was interesting and somewhat satisfying, but it was never my end all. I didn't prove my worth by my work.

Your biggest disappointments or regrets?

Really, no big disappointments. I definitely feel that I'm a lucky person.

Pat Pettit

recalls a mother whose meticulously detailed sewing was a way to make her daughter's dreams come true.

• • •

Dear Mother,

This year, being the hundredth anniversary of your birth, I wished to write of the memories that go through my mind. You were loved by many people, especially my father, sister and me.

You died 30 years ago today. A month after your death, my wonderful grandson arrived. The joy of holding him and talking to him eased the pain of losing you. A year later, his brother arrived, bringing with him a baby sister. These children are among the greatest joys of my life.

My granddaughter and I have spent many happy hours playing with my dolls. I kept the beautiful clothes you made for my dolls. After my granddaughter plays with them, she carefully places them back in the drawer where they stay safe for the next visit.

Your sewing is one of my most cherished memories. Many times before Christmas, I can remember peeking through the crack in the bedroom door and seeing you sewing into the night. I am so glad I saved these doll clothes and can touch their beautifully stitched lace and tiny ribbon rosebuds.

Sometimes I see a fashion show, like a kaleidoscope in my mind, featuring the lovely school clothes you made for me: most of all, one very special dress.

On November 11, 1934, we went downtown to buy a dress for me. (Yes, I remember this date so well, because when we returned from our shopping trip I discovered that my first period had started.)

The dress I liked best cost too much money. You suggested that we look for material and you would try to duplicate that dress. We chose the soft red woolen fabric. I can still feel it. The front opening was a 5- or 6-inch zipper. Zippers had been introduced only recently to home sewers. We went to the notions department to buy one, but it came only in white. The sales lady suggested that perhaps you could dye the zipper. Of course you could—and did.

I might have been the first little girl in the world to have a homemade dress with a zipper. That's not all! There was a little black Scotty dog on the breast pocket. That was no problem after you got a small piece of black felt, traced a Scotty dog from a coloring book, and carefully sewed it on my dress by hand.

Even now, thinking back about that special dress, I marvel how I can remember every detail. It must be the depth of my love for you. You will live forever in my heart.

PROFILE: Pat Pettit

Pat Pettit's house holds special meaning for her: Not only has she lived there for 57 years, but her husband built it. Her home is filled with works of art and crafts, each one carrying a story. As we talk, she shows me the doll clothes that her mother made for her. They are perfectly constructed, meticulously stitched, and clearly treasures.

Tell me about your work and your family.
I was a wife and mother. I'm 77. I was married to my husband, Richard, for 57 years. He died two years ago. I liked him a lot. *(She smiles.)* We had one son, who is 52. I have three grandchildren: two 29-year-old twins, and a boy who is 30. We're a close family; everyone lives in the area.

We ran a shop in Portland [Oregon]. Richard was a cabinetmaker, and I painted accessories, things like milk cans that became collectibles. The thing that happened was, over the years, various friends wanted me to refinish some of their furniture. They really liked my work, so I did more of it, and refinished furniture became part of the shop.

We intended to run the business until we died. But when my husband was 64, he had a brain hemorrhage and four brain surgeries. After that, he came back pretty well. But he did change in some ways. Before the surgery, he didn't want to go out to dinner. After the surgery, he wanted to go out a lot. We closed the shop and retired.

My husband could have died during the war and during brain surgery. God saved him for me. When he was 77, he had a second brain hemorrhage, and he did die. I surely didn't want him to be incompetent, and he wasn't. He went fast, in a week.

Why did you decide to write a Dear Mom letter?

Because my friend Claudia [Milazzo Hutchison] asked me. She is so precious.

I look back and I can't figure out how my mother knew the things she did. All her talents and graciousness.

My mother's name was Adelaide Weaver. Her own mother was 40 when my mother was born. My mother told me that my grandmother was a dynamo—working long hours at a small community newspaper they owned and then taking care of the house. My mother was sent to San Francisco State College to be a teacher, but then World War I broke out. My mother signed up to work for the Federal government and went to Washington, DC. She met my dad when he was stationed there as a soldier in the Army. My dad's family had a newspaper in Wisconsin.

Were there any surprises for you when you were writing your Dear Mom letter?

I was really surprised at how the letter just flowed, that it all came out.

I'm not surprised that I still miss my mom after 30 years. I think anybody would. Am I dwelling on it? No.

But after all this time, while writing the letter, I could hardly hold back my tears. The older I am, the more I realize how wonderful our family was.

How would you describe yourself now?

One thing very interesting happened as a result of my husband being in the hospital. After he died, I ended up volunteering at the hospital, doing clerical work two days a week. The CPR (cardiopulmonary resuscitation) rehabilitation unit honored me as a volunteer. They are so good to me. They tease me about being the matriarch of the exercise class.

Has your mother influenced you in the way you are a mother?

Yes. Everything had to be done right. My mother had high standards and I carried them on, maybe even to a fault. Our table manners had to be just so.

When I was growing up, my father was a building contractor, and my parents entertained beautifully. I think about the lovely parties and things they did together, they had such grace. How did they learn that? They just picked it up. My sisters and I had the advantage of learning from them.

What do you consider to be your biggest successes and accomplishments?

My everyday living is my best accomplishment, just being a good mom, wife, and friend. I haven't climbed any mountains or swum any rivers.

Your biggest disappointments or regrets?
I was taught not to dwell on regrets. Don't lament what you don't have: That's what my father taught me. So I don't think I have any regrets.

Paula Strange

takes a close look at the immeasurable debt she owes her mother.

• • •

Dear Mom,

You did a good job. What can I do to repay you?

• For being the kind of mother all my friends—to this very day—wish they had.

• For being the hub that our entire family revolves around.

• For giving me two brothers and two sisters whom I enjoy knowing in adulthood even more than I did in childhood.

• For giving me such a good role model of a successful marriage.

• For opening your home to everyone, anytime, for any reason.

• For cooking and cleaning and working so hard to prepare a beautiful home where everyone can enjoy time together.

What can I do to repay you?

• For the countless telephone calls on Saturday mornings that feed me spiritually. Those talks that always cut to the heart of the matter, feeling the connection between us, the appreciation of life, of books, of people. Swapping articles, stories, and real estate adventures, sharing so many things in a meaningful way. Starting the conversation with, "How was your week?" No one else asks me that.

What can I do to repay you?

• For learning not to give advice spontaneously but waiting until being asked.

• For your sensitivity and unconditional love.

• For your willingness to discuss nearly any topic.

• For your willingness to listen.

What can I do to repay you?

• For teaching me to "Write it down." "Follow your bliss." "Don't give up until you find what you're looking for." "Listen to your heart." "You'll figure it out." "You have great resourcefulness." "You can have whatever you want."

• For listening to all the "stumble stories": those times when I did not get what I wanted, and hit a dead end. The times when I felt hopeless—and cried.

What can I do to repay you?

• For taking an interest in my church and participating in it.

• For sharing the retreat in Crystal Mountain with Cecil and me, and supporting us when our marriage was difficult.

What can I do to repay you?

No single sum seems appropriate, although I still owe you money from the time you forgave a loan. You also freed me from a career that I was ready to leave emotionally, but unable to leave economically. You helped me to the next step: an important one on a journey to find work that provided a good living and satisfied my needs for diversity, independence, and meaningful human contact. (Isn't it funny that the destination I found was the one that you suggested years earlier?)

What can I do to repay you?

I don't know the answer. I would like you to tell me.

• • •

PROFILE: Paula Strange

Paula Strange meets me in the lobby of the hotel where I am staying in Portland, Oregon. She greets me in a friendly, businesslike manner. As we walk across the street to the restaurant, I try to imprint her appearance in my memory: She has short, reddish hair, an athletic build, and in her coordinated sportswear she looks very professional. Over breakfast, I ask her lots of questions about real estate, an interest of mine, and then we get down to the interview.

Tell me about your work and your family.

I'm 44, I've been married eight years, and I've been in real estate six years. I have two adult stepsons. One works in computer games, and the other is in college. Now I'm interested in becoming a mom myself.

I grew up in Des Moines, Iowa. When I was 17, my family went to Florida on a vacation. My older sister Peggy and I convinced our parents to let us stay for the entire summer if we found jobs. We became waitresses at the hotel restaurant and found a furnished apartment a few blocks away. We liked Florida so much that at the end of the summer we persuaded our entire family to move. I ended up going to college at Florida State.

Professionally, I've done lots of things. I have a communications degree, and after college I worked in advertising for several years. One summer I took a white-water rafting trip I loved, and that changed my life. I became a river guide in Idaho on the Salmon and Snake Rivers. I've also traveled a lot: to Europe, Egypt, and Israel.

Then I moved to Portland and worked for seven years as a travel agent, escorting groups on international trips.

I became restless and I went back to advertising. But I knew after a few years I needed a change. Mom suggested that I sell real estate. You can make a good living, and I really love my work as a realtor for Windermere Real Estate. You sell yourself and your services.

Why did you decide to write a **Dear Mom** *letter?*

I read an article a man wrote about the impact his mom had on his life. His mother had already passed away. I realized I wanted to write a letter to my mom while she was still alive.

Were there any surprises for you when you were writing your **Dear Mom** *letter?*

I don't think so.

How would you describe yourself now?

First and foremost, I'm an adventurer. I enjoy change and diversity. I've been that way all my life. I also work to improve myself. My mother encouraged this. She wanted me to get a good education so I could marry a doctor or lawyer. *(She says this with a big smile.)*

What does your husband do?

He's a lawyer. *(She laughs.)*

I have the job I want, the man I want, and the career I want. Now I know how my life turned out. The only part missing is a child. I don't want to move anymore, and I don't want to change careers. I'm pretty happy with my life.

I'm very fortunate in having a loving family, a close family. I was 16 when my parents divorced, but both are happily remarried. It's really nice that my mom knows how many lives she's touched. People tell me how wonderful it is to know my mom. Even her ex-daughters-in-law still have a relationship with her.

After I spend time with my mom, I feel like I'm a better person. She's 73 now.

When Mom turned 70, we had a party with a tribute to her. We sang that song, "You Are the Wind Beneath My Wings." We wanted her to know the impact she had on all of her children and other people, too.

Has your mother influenced you in wanting to be a mother?

Yes. I see how much her kids have enriched her life. She's given so much to us.

Is that something you want to emulate?

Yes. Now I have the energy and the time to give to a child. I always thought it would be enough to be a stepmother. But it's not. My mother is a great role model for how to be a mom. She always thinks that each person does her best. She doesn't remember bad things that happened—she forgets them.

I talked to my mother about how I would cope when she died. My mother said, "You will have such strength. All your brothers and sisters will support you, and it won't be so bad. That's how it was for me when my mother died."

What do you consider to be your biggest successes and accomplishments?

My biggest achievement is finding my soul mate. I never wanted to remarry, so I waited to find the right person, a sophisticated outdoorsman.

I also wanted to find a job I loved with a good salary; that's what I found in real estate.

I was always looking for a place that felt like home, and I found it in Portland. I live in a wonderful place I don't want to leave.

My plan was to travel in my 20s, get married and have children in my 30s, and write a book in my 40s.

It didn't turn out quite that way, but I'm happy. When I was 25, a friend gave me a poem about taking risks and experiencing life fully. That resonated with me, and that's how I try to live.

Your biggest disappointments or regrets?

The only disappointments I can think of are not getting into real estate earlier in my life, and waiting so long to have children.

Paula Strange's mother is Ruby Walker. Ruby's letter to her mom follows.

Ruby Walker

celebrates her mother's legacies of sunshine, security, and strength. She's especially grateful for the times her mother devised creative solutions to family problems.

• • •

Dear Mom,

You were an exceptional mother. I never ever told you how very special you were.

I never told you "Thank you" for the time you held my Peggy, all the way on that 80-mile race to the children's hospital in Omaha, Nebraska. I was soon to deliver our next baby, and I had no lap. On that midnight run, my little girl's temperature was 104, and I was so scared. You encouraged me all the way. I knew you were remembering when you lost your only baby boy at 6 months of age. You said to me, "Ruby, be thankful for the good doctors and hospital care they have now. You are winning your battle, and I lost mine." Those very words are still ruminating in my head, and even now, some 40 years later, they bring tears to my eyes.

Mom, I want to say "Thank you" for my good self-image. I know that I was not an easy child. Even when I was naughty, you never told me I was bad. Instead, you described me as headstrong.

You were a mother who understood the importance of childhood. I can still remember saying to you, "Mama, what can I do that's fun?" And you would hastily think of something to entertain me. You even let me drag out your extra table leaves to use as shelves in my make-believe store. We placed them from chair to chair and then stocked them with all the spices and canned goods I could get from your cupboards. You were the customer; I was the storekeeper, with a muffin pan to divide the pennies and nickels. I don't ever remember putting it all back. You must have done it after I was asleep.

Even though I was born in 1928 and grew up during the Depression, you never let me feel like we were poor. One year, we didn't have enough money to buy coal to heat our house on the Iowa farm. Instead, we burned our corn, which was 10 cents a bushel—cheaper than coal. So I'm sure there were times when we were broke. But we were never poor. We had books, and music that we played on our Victrola.

You were always positive, and had hope and faith. You loved our daddy, as did we all. One time I wrote you a letter saying, "The greatest gift a mother can give to her children is to love their daddy." You gave us that gift, and I am truly thankful!

You were so wise. You taught me to appreciate nature—not only the sunshine but also the rain. Remember the time you and I were a long way out in the field and it started to rain? I was 4 years old, and I started to cry. You said, "Oh, Ruby, don't cry when it rains. We need the rain for the crops to grow, and it falls so freely from the sky." And to this day, when it rains I say, "Thank you, God." One of your sayings has stayed with me all these years: "When there is no sunshine without, then we must make sunshine within."

Mom, you gave me such a feeling of security. Even after I was married, I knew that if anything bad happened beyond my control, you and Daddy would always make it all right. You were strong enough to let your children believe that Daddy was the "Rock of Gibraltar" in our lives. What a wonderful example you set for us.

Not until you died, six months before Daddy passed away, did we realize how much he gained his strength from you. And when you were no longer with us, Daddy fell apart and wanted every day to die. He would forget you died, and in the middle of the night he would call your name.

Thank you, Mom, for all your help with my two boys and three girls. They always knew that, if they could not get through to their dad or me, that they could always go to you and you would listen.

There were so many times your wisdom and caring helped us. I remember when my oldest, Russ, wanted us to move out to a small community so he could study vocational agriculture in high school. But we could not see the wisdom of uprooting our four younger children to satisfy one.

So Russ "ran away" from home. He drove 150 miles to you to plead his case and get your support. And you came up with a solution that was agreeable to all of us: Russ would live on a farm, work for his room and board, and go to a school where he could study vocational agriculture. With our permission, you even found him a farmer who needed help. Mom, you made a big difference in his life.

Sometimes, I hear my children quoting your sayings to their own kids:

"You are known by the company you keep."

"Beauty is only skin deep."

"You reap what you sow, tenfold, pressed down and running over."

It is clear that your sayings are being passed on from generation to generation.

All five of the children upon whom you put your mark are successful in life, not just financially. They are kind, good, and caring citizens of this great country. Much of their success today relates back to your loving influence. You gave them all unconditional love, and they are better people for that. Somehow I think you do know how well they are doing.

I wish I had told you earlier how very much I appreciated your guidance.

Profile: Ruby Walker

I contacted Ruby at the suggestion of her daughter, Paula Strange, another *Dear Mom* contributor. Ruby is 72, and has a voice full of energy. That she embraces life is clear in our conversation.

Tell me about your work and your family.

I grew up on a farm in southwestern Iowa. We were way out in the country; there was a dirt road to our place. I was the middle child. I needed playmates my own age, and the closest ones were two miles away. I was lonely.

When I started school, I loved it. I made some close friends. Every Memorial Day, we have our high school alumni banquet for Amity High School in College Springs, Iowa. And I try to go back each year. This will be our fifty-fifth year. We had only 22 in our class. We grew up together like brothers and sisters, and we have stayed in contact!

After high school, I got a job as a nurse's aide in a town nearby. I rented a room a block from the hospital. I worked strange hours, split shifts, and part of my pay was to have all my meals at the hospital.

Then the man with whom I had my first date came home from the Army. Every night we went out from 9 p.m. till 1 in the morning. I was 19 when I married him in 1947. I had been accepted at Swedish Lutheran Hospital for nurse's training, but I got married and didn't go for training.

I was married to him for 26 years. He's the father of my five children. I had all my kids within 10 years.

I don't have to ask you what you were doing—you were busy!

My husband worked as an auto mechanic. He was very good at that. When we got married, he didn't want me to work. He was very controlling. Then we moved to Missouri and had a farm. My father helped us buy the equipment. We worked the farm, and my husband drove a school bus. We were never poor, but we were broke.

I managed to stay married for 26 years. Then, when I was 45, I got divorced. I had to wait until my parents died before I divorced. My mother cried if any girl got a divorce. My daddy told me, "Divorce is worse than death. You just don't do it." If it hadn't been for that, I think I would have gotten divorced a lot sooner.

I had already started selling real estate. I felt like it was my turn, and my husband couldn't handle that at all. It wasn't his idea of a good wife.

I never planned to remarry. I realized that I didn't need marriage to be happy. I could make it on my own.

I loved my career. I met interesting people, and lots are still my friends.

Six months after my divorce, my kids and I all went on vacation to Florida. I had told my second son that if he ever got a 4.0 grade-point average in college, we would all go to Florida, and I would pay for the vacation.

So the summer of 1973, we went, with all five of my kids and the boys' two wives, and their babies. We hired a sitter for each baby.

Two of my daughters liked Florida so much, they decided to stay for the summer. They easily found jobs and an apartment, and had a wonderful summer. I went back to Iowa and realized that I didn't need those brutal winters anymore. Icy roads in Iowa were treacherous. So I decided, I'm going to work like hell so I can afford to move. I did, and we did. I put all my furniture in a trailer, and we went to Florida, without a job or a place to live.

That sounds like a big decision.

It was. I think I was divinely led. I was going to move to Daytona, but someone suggested I check out Sarasota. When I got there, I simply knew I was in the right place. So I got a job as a real estate agent, and my youngest daughter, Kathy, went to school there.

That's how I met my husband: He was my daughter's teacher! She was one of four girls in the construction class he taught. Her friends told him, "You should meet Kathy's mother." He called, and we talked for an hour. We both love farming. He was vice president of the Farm Bureau at the time. After two dates, I woke up my daughter Peggy and told her, "I'm going to marry Mr. Walker." On the third date, we decided to spend the rest of our lives together.

Six months later, we were married. And five years later, my daughter Peggy married Bill's son!

We moved to North Carolina six years ago. That's when I retired. Now two of my daughters sell real estate: Paula in Portland, Oregon, and Kathy in Sarasota, Florida.

Why did you decide to write a **Dear Mom** *letter?*
Because I was so thrilled with what my daughter Paula wrote and sent to me. I think Paula suggested that I write my own letter. You know, my mother had a big influence on all my kids. I had the only grandchildren, and my mother was elated with my two boys and three girls.

Were there any surprises for you when you were writing your **Dear Mom** *letter?*
I can't read it without crying.

Because you still miss her?
No, it just brings back so many memories. I always had my parents for support. I really grew up after my mother and daddy died. Last July, my Paula said to me, "I just can't imagine you dying." I told her, "It will be okay. You will be strong, and you have a lot of good memories."

Did you know what you were going to write?
No, I really didn't know until I had my pen in my hand. The words just flowed out of my pen.

How would you describe yourself now?
Together and complete.

My husband, Bill Walker, is one in a million. He had been married for 25 years and was divorced when we met. At that time, I had had two years of being single since my divorce. That's when I really got it together. I know now that even if Bill died, I could make it on my own, and he knows the same thing. After we'd been married three years, I told him I only had one worry— that his first wife would want him back, and he might go. He told me that wouldn't happen. We each know we can make it on our own. We're together because we want to be. We're not trapped.

My first husband is now remarried. And we're all very good friends. The kids appreciate that. I just don't believe in being unhappy.

Has your mother influenced you in the way you are a mother?

Oh yes. Being a mother is the most important job in the world. People go to school for years to do something far less important.

My mother surely gave us a great sense of security. She was wonderful and caring, and all the kids were close to her and my dad.

My mother saved my sanity when my children were little and we didn't have electricity. I washed my clothes at my mother's house. At first, living on the farm, we just had an outdoor toilet. Then my dad and first husband added a bathroom.

My two boys were competitive and would fight, and that was hard for me to deal with. So my mother would take one of the boys for a week at a time and take care of him. Then the other boy would say, "Please let him come back." My mother had three daughters; her only son died at six months. She told me, "Be careful that the boys don't become enemies." What we did, worked. Today, my boys are good friends.

What do you consider to be your biggest successes and accomplishments?

(She answers without hesitation.) My five kids. They're absolutely wonderful.

Another thing I consider a great success concerns my youngest child, Kathy. When she was 5 years old, she was diagnosed with juvenile diabetes. I didn't want her to become emotionally crippled because she had a disability. I'd seen that happen to other children, and I vowed we would not let this happen to our Kathy. At age 9, she learned to give her own insulin shots. When she did become discouraged, her brothers and sisters would stop whatever they were doing and zero in on her problem. She had a lot of family support, so I did not do it alone, but I claim her as a big success story.

Today, as an adult, Kathy plays tennis, and she is a member of the Juvenile Diabetes Board in Sarasota, Florida. In March of 2000 she was appointed by the governor to sit on the Florida Diabetic Council. They are trying to get more government funds for diabetic research. More people die of diabetes each year than die of breast cancer and AIDS combined. Yet much fewer government funds go to research to find a cure for diabetes.

Your biggest disappointments or regrets?

My biggest regret: I had one big basket of letters I had written to my mother and father when my kids were little, and when I moved, they somehow disappeared.

If I had my life to live over, I would still get married at 19, have five babies, get divorced 26 years later, and marry Bill Walker.

Paula Strange is Ruby Walker's daughter. Paula's letter to Ruby precedes Ruby's to her mother.

Joan Ingram

honors a mother who gave her daughter a childhood far more loving and secure than her own.

• • •

My dearest Mom,

When I was growing up, a friend of mine once said, "If all mothers were like yours, what a happy world this would be."

We have never been a family to express our love and caring in words, only in actions. Not until you were on your deathbed did I say, "I love you."

But you were always a nurturing presence in my life. I remember you tucking me into bed every night until I married at 21. You were always there for me when I was upset or ill. You put a hot water bottle in the foot of my bed on cold winter nights to comfort me. You never made us eat anything we didn't care for, always putting delicious food before us.

When I asked you once why you named your only daughter such a plain name, your response was, "Dear, I named you after Joan of Arc. I hoped only that you should be so courageous. And you are." This had to be one of the few compliments you ever paid me; but then again, you rarely criticized me.

Mom, I have followed your lessons and your example: You taught me not to cry over spilt milk, but to make sure the next effort would be without failure. You taught me never to go to bed angry and that each day was a new beginning. You taught me to listen to my conscience. There were times when I felt headstrong about doing something and you would say, "Dear, you may do it if you want, but remember that I don't approve." Consequently, on things I didn't consider very important, I would acquiesce.

Yes, Mom, we did have our disagreements, but we never held animosities. Sometimes you gave me advice that I did not intend to heed—nor did I. I know you desperately wanted me to have the education you never had. You sent me to Catholic boarding school for my senior year of high school so I would get a better education and more exposure to the arts. Then I met my Dal and wanted to marry him. That was the end of my schooling—a major disappointment for you, but you accepted my decision.

I know my friends thought I acquiesced to you too easily, but I could be very definite about what I truly wanted. I remember, even naming my children was quite a struggle—you had your own ideas! But I won out. I knew you would accept my decisions once they were made. Mom, I appreciated that so much.

You loved being needed. You made all of our wool quilts, feather pillows, crocheted doilies, hooked rugs, braided rugs, potholders, tea towels, and many other beautiful things that we still admire in our homes today.

You grew a wonderful organic vegetable garden with three fruit trees, some strawberries, and a wonderful raspberry patch. Your pies and jams were so tasty that we still remember them.

During those long days with Dal out at sea, you were my inspiration, always willing to talk and encourage me. I enjoyed your company so much. You were well-read, politically astute, creative, artistic, and emotionally stable. After working outside in the garden, I would catch the smell of fresh bread coming from the oven and you would call me in for tea and bread.

You were such an important force in the lives of your grandchildren—inspiring, guiding, and encouraging them. Mom, even though you are gone, you are still a presence in their lives.

Now, at 73 and having been without you for seven years, I fully realize how exceptional you were. You gave me the childhood, security, and opportunities you never had.

I only wish I'd told you how enormously proud of you I was. But I console myself by reflecting that my own life is true to your powerful example.

At this stage of my life, I like myself, and after 53 years of marriage, my husband still loves me. I cherish my four children and five grandchildren. God willing, your guidance, devotion, and love will pass on through the coming generations.

We all miss you. What an admirable legacy you've left behind. Thank you, Mom, from the bottom of my heart.

PROFILE: Joan Ingram

Joan's home includes several acres on Salt Spring Island in British Columbia, Canada. Everywhere, there is something to delight the senses: the smell of roses, the sounds of birds and nearby farm animals, the entrancing sight of light dancing on the ever-present water. It is truly a magical place.

Joan's contemporary home is decorated with her paintings. We talk in the bright open kitchen. The smell of something wonderful in the oven floats through the room.

Tell me about your work and your family.
My husband, Dal, worked as a commercial fisherman. Fishing is a very dangerous profession. It's a life that can be terrible, but it also can be good. You need to be prepared, cautious, and well-equipped. Dal had a crew of five, and he worked all year-round. He caught salmon, whitefish, and cod.

Like all commercial fishermen, Dal was gone a lot. He would be home for Christmas and New Year's, and usually the month of June, but maybe all together he was home for two months of the year. Women married to fishermen must be very self-sufficient.

I come from a fishing family: My father and grandfather were fisherman, and we always had boats for work and for fun. So I knew what to expect.

I lived at home until I was married. My mother put a great emphasis on education, but I didn't want to go to college. I only wanted to get married.

I was 19 when Dal and I got engaged, and we were married when I was 21. We eloped! But my parents loved Dal. He was everything they wanted in a son-in-law. We've been married 53 years, and I'm still in love with my husband.

I've been very lucky—blessed with good parents and a good life. I think I was born under a lucky star. I'm very family oriented. I have four children and five grandchildren, and I love seeing them.

Why did you decide to write a Dear Mom letter?

The main reason is that I am so proud of my mother. She told me a lot about her childhood, and I still cry when I think of what she went through and what she made of her life.

My mother, Irene Stevens-Sileck, was born right here on Salt Spring Island in 1899. She was the sixth child in a family of eight. Her mother was Emma King, a Coast Salish Native and her father was John (Yanaris) Stevens, a Greek immigrant sailor. When Irene was about six years old, her parents separated. Emma took Irene back to her native Songhees village in Victoria, BC.

Emma started another family of six more children— and my mother became the caregiver. Her gentle and devoted father had taught her responsibilities, morals, and a keen desire to learn. Although she had no formal education, she taught herself to read and write.

Emma was stern and demanding; she gave little thought to hitting my mom with a stick. Being treated that way made my mother abhor cruelty and violence. When Mom was only 9, she was put to work at the fish cannery in Victoria, stacking cans and at times gathering seaweed off the rocks for the Japanese market. When I heard about this, the work sounded dangerous and hard. But my mother was capable, and to her, this was normal.

When Mom was in her early teens, her life changed for the better. She went to live with her father and six brothers who were commercial fisherman on the Fraser River in British Columbia. She told me it was there, on Dease Island, that she found kindness and caring. She was living in a small Greek community where the women encouraged her and taught her to cook and sew. She also sang beautifully. She was a classic beauty, with high cheekbones, Greek features, black-brown eyes, and silky blue-black hair.

On the island there were dances and musical evenings that she enjoyed immensely. She met and fell in love with her handsome, strong, future husband, my father, Mitchell Sileck. Courtship was not easy under the stern eye of her father and six brothers, who, even though they approved of her choice, did not want to lose their house-keeper.

Finally, Mitch grew tired of waiting and said, "Now or never." This ultimatum prompted her to accept his offer of marriage. They were married right here on Salt Spring Island, in 1925.

My parents had two children: myself and my brother. Both Mom and Dad were loving and devoted. Growing up, I watched my mother extend a helping hand whenever it was needed. She was the only person in the community who held a Saint John's Ambulance certificate and therefore was called upon for various emergencies and illnesses.

Mom was very wise. When I was a teenager, she told me, "I'm not going to allow you to date, but you can have your friends in the house." We would play the piano and eat Mom's great food. During the war, I had soldiers at the house all the time, and they always treated me with respect. Mom was right there!

Even after I married, I was very close to my mom. With Dal gone so much, she and I would sit around the table and talk about everything. Much later, after my father died, she came to live with us. She was a wonderful influence on my children.

Before she died, at 93, she told me, "I've had a good life, a good husband, good children. My only regret is not having gone to school."

Were there any surprises for you when you were writing your Dear Mom letter?

Maybe the only one is that I got to know myself and my mother better, just by writing the letter.

DEAR MOM

How would you describe yourself now?

(She smiles, laughs.) How would I describe myself! I'm not disappointed in myself; now *that's* my mother's influence.

Neurotic? *(She laughs).*

Really, I'm contented. At 73, I still have hopes of doing lots of things. I enjoy my painting.

I only want to go places to see my kids and grand-children.

Has your mother influenced you in the way you are a mother?

Yes, she influenced me. My morals came from her and my church.

Sometimes, we did have some friction. She was very cautious, and that made it harder for me to let the kids have fun.

Pretty well she influenced everything I did. She was always close by. At least twice a week, we went to her place for dinner. My mother would stay with us when the kids were sick. She helped me in so many ways.

What do you consider to be your biggest successes and accomplishments?

Raising my family, and being a good wife.

Your biggest disappointments or regrets?

Well, I'm disappointed I didn't inspire my children to

develop their talents in music and art—because they are gifted in those areas.

My only regrets about a life such as I had, being married to a commercial fisherman, are the isolation and loneliness at night and early mornings. The days were always busy and full, and the children kept life exciting and also rewarding. Such closeness seems to be missing in today's families.

Claudia Milazzo Hutchison

carries her late mother's voice inside her. Sitting at her kitchen table, she draws strength from the powerful inner message, "You can do hard things."

• • •

Dear Mom,

Tomorrow is Mother's Day. My family is out shopping, no doubt concocting some surprise for tomorrow—a brunch in bed, a floral arrangement, coupons promising to do all those chores I've been nagging about.

Ah, household chores—the universal bugaboo of family life. I can still hear your words so clearly.

"The appearance of your bedroom is your decision."

"Close the door to your room; we're having company." No nagging. No guilt trips. How I wish I had the grace to mimic your equilibrium.

Now I sit at the kitchen table, composing a last letter to you. I am bursting with the fragments of my life that I want to share with my mother—the events you have missed these past four months: Jacob studying for a semester in London; Christine playing Prokofiev in the honors recital. And Mom, Don and I have finally taken that long-planned trip to Italy!

To whom does a daughter "tell her stuff" when her mother is gone? To whom does she brag about her children?

"You tell your children directly how wonderful they are," advises my wise, older friend Nancy, who has been motherless for several years. I do, but nothing can replace our weekly phone chats and the reassuring warmth of your voice—or our less-frequent marathon face-to-face catch-ups across the kitchen tables, yours and mine, over the years.

So I sit down to write one last Mother's Day letter to you. One last Mother's Day gift, in the form of a promise: a promise to remember you every day. To remember all of your life: not to focus on the last several years when you became increasingly frail and confused. A promise to remember the whole and the essence of you.

I reread your younger sister Olga's condolence letter, about happy times when you played the piano with your college girlfriends. I had read it earlier to my family.

"I didn't know Grandma played piano. What kind of songs did she play?" my daughter wanted to know.

Now I close my eyes and remember. I see three young children—myself, big brother Eddie, and little Larry, marching about our apartment to the beat of "Sur le Pont d'Avignon." Your love of languages was reflected in our knowing all the words to "Au Clair de la Lune" and "Frère Jacques"—without having a clue to their meaning! Songs of travel and faraway places filled our young imaginations.

"April in Portugal" I remember one song is called. I give up after a few futile attempts to recall the words. But later that week they come to me unaware, simply and clearly, just as my childhood dreams came, transported on the breeze through our open living room window on those summer afternoons in Brooklyn so long ago. I close my eyes and again feel the sticky August air on my face. I glimpse your sturdy back and upright posture; I hear the soft crinkling swoosh of your powder-blue crinoline sundress against the piano bench. Your chestnut waves shimmer at the nape of your neck as you and the piano sing together.

These long-ago scenes are vivid as I sit here alone at the proverbial kitchen table. What memories and reassurances a simple piece of furniture can conjure. Our memories grew around a Formica-topped rectangular table, surrounded by four white wrought-iron chairs; the step stool, which doubled as a seat when we all ate together, pushed off to the side. It seems odd to me now that despite the spacious dining room in our Brooklyn apartment, the five of us shared our weekday dinners cramped into the tiniest room in the house.

My seat was wedged between my little brother (on the step stool) and the window, through which I'd glance past the fire escape toward the apartments across the courtyard. You sat next to the stove, so you could dish out the savory minestrone and overcooked broccoli directly from pots to plates. A cramped old kitchen in an old New York City apartment building, where of necessity the table doubled as a work surface. So small, so simple, so inviting.

In this same apartment, a playful 8-year-old, costumed in oversized high heels and bedecked with stands of artificial pink pearls, pushes a miniature baby stroller down the hallway.

"Knock knock." I rap at the doorway of the kitchen. I'm bringing my daughter to visit her grandma.

"Come in, come in!" Your melodic voice welcomes me. "Put your baby in the highchair." I drag "Tiny Tears Teresa" from her wrappings and prop her against the drain board while you prepare a pretend snack for her. We sing "Ciao, Ciao, Bambina" as you roll out ravioli dough on the kitchen table.

My memories fast-forward. I'm now encased in my room, when I'm not at junior high. The thump-be-bop of my records blares throughout the apartment when you open my now always-closed door. You call me into the kitchen. You sit at the table, but I park myself on the step stool. I leave it pushed back into the corner—the farthest position in the room I can find from you. I avoid looking at you, but I still feel the consternation of your steady brown eyes through your horn-rimmed bifocals. I gaze over the top of your brown head, relishing my increased height and superiority.

The years flash by. Now I see you tossing olive oil and vinegar into an iceberg lettuce salad when I come in with my high school biology text. You quiz me on the endocrine system, but I'm confused and complain that it's hard.

You state, simply and indisputably, *"You can do hard things."* Then you wipe your hands on the dishtowel, pull a chair alongside of mine, and together we peer at the diagrams. I note raised blue veins and puckering knuckles as you point at the various diagrams and captions.

A few years later: I am home on winter break from the state university. Even though it's late when I return from a party, I find you awake, seated at the kitchen table with an untouched cup of tea. Your gray-flecked hair is twisted into coils held tightly against your scalp by brown metal bobby pins. Your slouching body is clothed in the checked housedress I used to dread finding you in when I returned home unannounced with friends.

You look up and you see right away that I have been crying. You ask me what's wrong. I tell you the evening with my boyfriend did not go well, and I don't think I'll be seeing him much longer.

You say you've had a hard evening also, and now I notice a redness about your eyes. You tell me that Dad's "minor surgery" last spring was "exploratory surgery." That the diagnosis was "cancer—terminal." In my shocked numbness, I barely register your next comment: You say you don't think we'll be seeing him much longer either.

Sadly, Mom, you were correct. My father lived only two more months, and I saw him only twice more on quick trips home. But fortunately I was wrong about my boyfriend. After returning to our separate colleges, we managed to mend our relationship, and marry almost immediately upon graduation. Even as a young bride, I spent many happy times visiting you, sometimes with Doug and sometimes alone, sharing meals and talks.

Our significant conversations as well as mundane chats all occurred in the cramped Brooklyn kitchen amid the yellowing paint, the refrigerator's hum, and the undergarments suspended by wooden clothespins from the drying apparatus hung overhead.

• • •

I can't recall the appearance of the kitchen table in the tiny Nevada apartment Doug and I rented when we moved away from Brooklyn two years into our marriage. But, Mom, I do remember many phone calls to you while seated at the table in that room. Reports of Doug's doctors' visits, of chemotherapy side effects, of unknowns.

I think you told me once or twice then, as you had in the past, *"You can do hard things."*

I don't recall many of the details of those traumatic months. But I do clearly remember an urgent phone call to you. By telling me that you would be on the next cross-country flight, you gave me the connection to life that I needed to survive those agonizing first few hours of young widowhood.

You remained with me in Nevada for one week. After you left, I returned to my teaching job. When the school year ended, I fled home to Brooklyn—to you—to regain my equilibrium. Again, hours of sharing confidences and mending hearts occurred in moments together over tea in your kitchen.

• • •

Now, on this afternoon before Mother's Day, I sit in my Oregon kitchen and gaze out the window to the greenery and the backdrop of the Northwest Cascades. I remember how much you loved this view.

You started visiting me in Portland over 20 years ago. First you came to scrutinize Don and Micol, the man and his daughter who had won my heart. Next you came to attend our wedding, and you just couldn't resist coming once more before Jacob's birth to see me pregnant.

I close my eyes and recall your earliest visits here. With my infant son dozing in my arms, I sit at the antique oak table scanning the newspaper. The teapot begins to boil, and as if on cue, you rush in from another part of the house.

"Just stay right there," you said. "I'll take care of it."

I did a lot of just staying and letting you take care of things when you visited during those years.

Another time: I am seated alone at the kitchen table. I am weak and exhausted, having just returned home from the maternity ward. Don hands me the phone. I key in your phone number. I tell you that we named her Beth. That she was beautiful. That she weighed just over 1 pound. That she was perfectly formed.

LOVE

A long silence. Then, "Try not to be too sad," you gently advise me.

• • •

Over the next several years, declining health makes your visits less frequent. But one summer I convince you to come. After a stiff, slow walk from the guest room, you sit hunched over your plate of pasta primavera. The arthritis has progressed so rapidly you can't even reach your trembling thin hand up far enough to replace a wayward strand of hair. Tomorrow I will take you for your first experimental DMSO (dimethyl sulfoxide) treatment. When the meal is over, you apologize for not getting up to help clear. You are too weak.

Just four months later, you have made a miraculous recovery. I have a vibrant mother once more. We have just returned from the Christmas Eve church service. The children have gone to bed, and Don is upstairs, wrapping gifts. You and I shape into bows the ribbons of pastry we rolled out earlier for "Gnocchi da Regina." We fry them in boiling oil. Then we stand side by side at the counter to drain them on paper towels, drizzle them with honey, and set them on dessert platters. Your fresh-scented silvery hair sweeps softly against my cheek as you turn. Your touch and your scent and the fragrance of warm honey envelop me in a brief moment of indescribable happiness. The image conjured by the minister's words of an hour ago fills my heart: He had spoken of a fantasy to be present at the first Christmas, to feel only the joy, without the knowledge of the pain yet to come.

The years fast-forward. The children are teens and preteens. You are less mobile. Still, you come to visit when you can.

You enter my kitchen and see that something is dreadfully wrong. The five of us are holding each other, the children sobbing, my husband ghostly pale. An early-morning phone call. A car accident. My brother-in-law, only 29, instantly dead. Several mornings that week I find you seated at the kitchen table with one of your grandchildren, whispering shared confidences, offering encouragement. How I appreciate your presence to help me support my pained family.

The years rush on. You are now frail and elderly, in need of daily assistance. But my brothers and I finally convince you to come to Portland for an extended stay.

An arrangement of daisies on the table reflects the summer morning's sunshine. I am mixing batter for blueberry pancakes. The slow, methodical clunking of your walker, interspersed with the dragging of your bedroom slippers across my hardwood floors, announces your approach. You pause by the dishwasher to catch your breath. Then you reposition your walker and maneuver your stooped frame into your place at my kitchen table. You tell me the pancakes are delicious. The hearty, bellowing laughter of "those two Italian mechanics" (Tom and Ray Magliozzi) we listen to on the radio on Saturday mornings brings a slight smile to your now often downcast countenance. You have so few pleasures these days.

• • •

Now over a year has passed, and I am looking forward to my upcoming New York visit to celebrate your eighty-sixth birthday. I have just returned from shopping; I am standing right here at my kitchen table sorting groceries when my daughter calls out, "Uncle Ed's on the phone." Two hours later, I am on a flight, and 10 hours later, I am in a Brooklyn hospital. My brothers, my sister-in-law, and I keep vigil at your bedside.

Exhausted by my travel and by the unknowns of your situation, I teeter on the edge of breaking down. It is all so hard.

"You can do hard things," the mother voice within my head reminds me.

On the third day, from a semiconscious state, you stir and mumble, slowly open one eye, and then speak. Between incoherent mutterings come occasional clear phrases. Suddenly both eyes flutter open. Seated by your bedside, I position my face just inches from yours. You know I am right there, beside you. You say my name. As we gaze into each other's eyes, I recognize the look you give me. I have seen it before.

Wordsworth tells us that babies come into the world "trailing clouds of glory." A newborn has a certain fleeting look that tells the world he has come from somewhere, that she knows something, that he is wise. The aura of aged wisdom lasts only momentarily, and then the newborn quickly acquires the look of a baby. Just a baby. The newborn and the mother gaze into each other's eyes with such intensity; the mother falls in love with her child forever. She knows in that instant that she would go to the ends of the earth for him; that she would walk through fire to keep her safe.

It is this same look I see in your eyes at this moment in your hospital room. You and I are falling in love with each other again. I know in this instant that we have shared this look once before. Now it is you who are vulnerable and I who must keep you safe.

Later that day you become agitated and uncomfortable. Instinctively I start to sing. My voice seems to calm you, so I continue. With little conscious effort, the songs of my childhood are summoned forth—"Que Sera, Sera," "Au Clair de la Lune," and many others that you taught me so long ago. You doze peacefully.

The next day you speak more clearly, but your illogical statements indicate that you are already entering another world.

"Alfred, Alfred," you intermittently call out my father's name. Are you in your kitchen, calling him to dinner? Are you on a grassy hillside in Woodlawn, bidding a final goodbye?

"Alfred, Alfred." I am awestruck by the quality of your love, a love not silenced even after a 30-year absence—even as all systems shut down.

The next day you are fading. Your mumbling becomes incoherent. Your breathing is shallow. The doctor says you are not in pain. But you are so weak and fidgety. I am reminded of a bird I once saw flopping about on the sidewalk. I look at you and see that you have become that bird with a broken wing, a bird that will not rise and fly again. My heart is breaking and I cannot stop weeping. I flee from the hospital room. I telephone my husband. I want Don to tell me that I'm not a bad daughter if I can't stay with you now. It's just too hard. He reassures me, but then it is your voice that I hear, through the telephone line.

Your mantra for my life: *"You can do hard things."*

I return to your room.

• • •

The following week, our family is once again gathered on the grassy hillside in Woodlawn, a much smaller assembly than in former years. The gravesite no longer stands alone on an empty hill, as it did so long ago, but is now crowded by surrounding headstones. Only minutes earlier the snow had started to fall, and already the ground is lightly covered. With the back of my gloved hand, I wipe away snow from the headstone so that we can read my father's name—and see the place next to his where your name will be engraved.

The snow is unceasing. Huge white flakes decorate the bronzed roses on your white casket. Today would have been your eighty-sixth birthday. "Happy birthday in heaven," your sister Mary whispers as she places her rose on your coffin and turns to leave.

It is my turn to offer a final goodbye. As I place my flower upon your casket, I recall the last lines of a poem I wrote after my father died so long ago. Did I ever share it with you?

> *The tear-streaked face of an aging wife*
> *leans on the shoulder of a now grown son.*
> *Lingering petals of a withering bloom*
> *fall listlessly from a daughter's hand*
> *onto a father's tomb.*

Tomorrow I will write a poem for you as well.

• • •

Four months have now passed since your death. When friends express sympathy, I tell them it is better this way. You wouldn't have wanted to live in the condition that the stroke would have left you. You had become so frail, and you were no longer able to enjoy any aspect of your life. Your mind, once so sharp, was oftentimes confused. After one of our last phone conversations, I told myself that one day soon I would call and you wouldn't know who I was. I thank God we were spared all that.

I have spent four months saying it is better this way— four months of rationalizing away the pain, of not allowing myself to feel nor remember it fully.

To remember what a wonderful mother you were makes it harder to say goodbye. To remember that you were the one person whose faithful and unconditional love I have been able to count on, for five decades of my life, deepens the pain.

And now, on Mother's Day eve, seated at the kitchen table, my tears begin to flow. Because now I am finally allowing myself to remember. To remember all aspects of you.

And now I even remember the last verse to "April in Portugal." Through my sniffles, I hum it to myself. Your brown curls are aglow before my closed eyes as you sit at the piano, your melodic voice filling the small apartment, and me, a happy free child once more, dancing pirouettes behind you.

Suddenly my tears fall unabashedly, releasing the sorrow I have kept in check.

But then I hear you. You are coming to comfort me. You rush into the kitchen as the teapot begins to boil. You bring my just-awakened baby for me to nurse. You push your walker and drag your crippled feet into my kitchen to sit with me and chat over a cup of tea.

"You can do hard things," you tell me. "Try not to be too sad."

The heart has limits to how much loss it can endure. I feel beaten down. I don't know if I can still do hard things. But I will try not to be too sad.

And I will always remember you.

PROFILE: Claudia Milazzo Hutchison

Claudia Hutchison's letter made me cry the first time I read it. And several times thereafter. After many emails and telephone conversations, I am glad to meet her in person. We talk over lunch in downtown Portland.

Tell me about your work and your family.
I'm a 48-year-old, second-generation, Italian-American transplant from the East to West Coast. I have been married to my husband Don for almost 24 years, mostly quite happily. Together we have a blended family of four children, now all young adults—and one grandchild! Our oldest son and his wife have a baby girl. And our youngest, our daughter, is getting ready to go to college.

My first career was teaching in high schools and community colleges. My current career is in domestic special-needs adoptions. First I recruited families to adopt children in state care and now I direct a resource center for these families.

Why did you decide to write a **Dear Mom** *letter?*
I wrote my letter to help me preserve and share with my family an image of my mother, Felicetta—"Etta." During the last few years of her life, Etta, like many frail elderly, became increasingly negative and unhappy. I really didn't want that to be the memory I hung onto, because the person she became during those last years was not a true reflection of who she was.

Were there any surprises for you when you were writing your Dear Mom letter?

Yes. I worked on the letter for a few days, but pulled most of it together the day before Mother's Day. The whole ending of the letter was a surprise to me. Several times during the writing, I was interrupted by uncontrollable sobbing, followed by a sense of release. I was able to calm myself by feeling my mother's spirit still hovering around me. And as I did so, I gave myself permission to let go of the more recent memories of her negativity, and to remember Etta as she was for most of her life—engaging, positive, and supportive. She was interested in and concerned about other people. She did hard things, too—without calling attention to them.

How would you describe yourself now?

I'm a fairly balanced midlifer, ready to be an empty nester, entering my 50s, and looking forward to the next chapter to see what unfolds before me. I love being a mom, a grandma, and an adopted aunt for friends' children. I love all that, but I'm looking forward to being done with full-time parenting. I want to have some "honeymoon" time alone with my husband, because we have never been together without children in our family. (In fact, this is the sixteenth consecutive year of our having at least one teenager at home!) I want to see what direction my life takes me. I know I'll continue to be involved with children and families in some yet-undefined way.

Has your mother influenced you in the way you are a mother?

Etta was a good listener, and when it came to the really important issues, she was nonjudgmental. I strive for that, because it's not always easy.

What would be a really important issue? Can you give me an example?

Oh, a person struggling with sexual orientation. Or an intercultural relationship. These were significant obstacles in her generation and family, but she was always pretty accepting.

Both my parents were foreign-language teachers, and they loved traveling. We lived in a modest apartment in New York City. We didn't have a lot of money or possessions, but my parents exposed us to everything the city had to offer: Broadway plays, museums, all of it.

Sometimes my brothers or I would say we didn't want to do something. My parents would say to each other, "You don't ask them if they want to go. They're too young to make that decision. It's the parents' job to expose them to…" art, literature, whatever.

Don and I have followed that example of trying to expose our children to travel, culture, and the arts as much as possible. (That is probably why our children have majored in philosophy, theater, and languages!)

What do you consider to be your biggest successes and accomplishments?

My successes have come in pairs: two college degrees, two careers, two marriages, two children born to me, two more children I was lucky enough to help raise, and having twice celebrated milestone birthdays by swimming across the Columbia River from Washington to Oregon—1.2 miles!

Seriously, my proudest accomplishments are my marriage and my family. When I met Don, I was a new widow and he had recently divorced—not the ideal time for either of us to start a new relationship. But I quickly recognized in him the qualities I value in a man: stability, intelligence, compassion, warmth, humor— and he can cook! I was so impressed with his devotion to his daughter, and I saw the potential for a great family life together. We can't always control the timing of life's gifts. We have to be brave enough to grab them when they come along.

I am most proud of our four children. They are all incredibly wonderful young adults. I can't imagine anything more rewarding than that.

Your biggest disappointments or regrets?

I really don't think I have any. My husband comes from a family whose philosophy is that you don't look back, and I think a bit of that outlook has rubbed off on me over the years.

Women's
letters
of loss

Pat Pierson

longed to rescue her loving and much-loved mother from Pat's abusive father. Decades after losing her mother, Pat's agonizing questions linger.

• • •

Dear Mother,

What I was trying to tell you in my last letter was, don't give up. Just wait for me. I have a plan.

If you could just persuade him to move here, near me, together we could resist his power over you. I could stand up to him now.

I understand so many things now that I'm grown. When I was a child, you hid so much from me. I had no idea how bad life was for you. You must have put all your thoughts and energy into creating a safe, happy environment for your children. I want you to know that in spite of the scary times with him, you did it, Mom.

As I've grown older and raised my own children, I realize more and more what a truly remarkable job you did with what you had to work with.

I remember asking you one time if we were poor. Your response was, "Do you think we are?" To this day I have never figured it out. I know now that we barely got by, but then, so did most of our neighbors. The funny thing is, though, we were raised differently from the other kids.

You read to us every night. You made us use table manners, and you taught us to appreciate classical music. I still have the poem you wrote for me on my ninth birthday. The one in which you said I was a treasure, a gift from God to you.

I guess I'm just in the mood to tell you that the special things you did for me didn't go unnoticed. I realize now that not every mom would let her kids have a pet goat and a rabbit—especially when they both wanted to be house pets. Nor would they have let me cash in my precious savings bond to buy majorette boots when my only school shoes were falling apart.

You were so wise, Mom. You realized that the prom dresses and majorette boots were more important than sensible shoes and decent underwear.

All those thoughtful things you did for me showed me how much you loved me, even though I can't remember your actually saying it. Your love gave me the sense of security I needed to build my own life.

As I said, I understand so much now, and have wanted to make it up to you for all your unhappiness. Still, as I write this, I don't understand what you did.

Why, Mother?

Why couldn't you wait for me?

Why a shotgun?

Profile: Pat Pierson

When I first read Pat Pierson's letter, I felt like someone had punched me in the stomach. And I felt compelled to find out more about her and her mother.

Tell me about your work and your family.
I'm 68 years old now.

How old were you when your mom committed suicide?
I was about 38.

My mom was 59 when she killed herself. My father was very controlling, and my mother really needed to escape. Later, after she died, I found out that he had been physically as well as emotionally abusive. He played a lot of mind games. He also threatened her with a gun, and he told her if she ever left, he'd kill her.

What happened to your father?
About a year and a half after she died, he remarried his former sweetheart. He died in 1976.

Tell me about you.
I've had a very exciting life—some good, some bad.

My mother was pregnant with me when my 2-year-old sister was killed in a car wreck. My mother was the driver, and she never got over it. She devoted her life to my younger brother and me. My brother and I love each other dearly.

I grew up in San Diego, and lived in California till I was 21. As a child, I was afraid of my father, but I remember him actually hurting me only a couple of times. My mother would send me to the neighbors to protect me.

I met my first husband in college where he was studying to be a minister. We married when I was 21 and moved to Georgia. We were married for 20 years, had two children, and then divorced.

I was heartbroken. It was the first of a decade of tragedies to come, each of which I thought would kill me.

During the 1970s, my mother committed suicide. My husband lost all our money, left me for another woman, and then died. Worst of all, my beautiful, talented, 16-year-old daughter was killed in a car accident.

Thinking I could escape the grief of these losses, I went to Europe for several years, where I taught in a fashion college and in time became dean of students.

I was living in London when I found out that my ex-husband's second marriage had broken up. From things he told my son, I thought maybe we had a chance to get back together. Then, before anything could happen, he had a brain aneurysm and died in his sleep at age 44.

My son was 25, so he was grown, but he had lost his sister and his father, and I knew I should be with him. Out of what had been a family of four, only the two of us were left.

Those were the bad things.

Now here is a good thing: About a year before my daughter's accident, her best friend came to live with us, and I became her guardian. I loved her from the start. God is merciful, and Carol has filled the painful void left by the loss of my daughter. Miraculously, she and my son fell in love, and four years later got married. They're still married. They are a bright spot in my life.

Upon returning to Atlanta, I started a design and manufacturing business specializing in bridal and formal wear; I called it Patricia Green Couture—my name being Patricia Green at the time.

Eventually, I met the man who became my second husband. I married him, and we moved to Utah. After five months of marriage, he had a cardiac arrest and then was diagnosed with cancer. His last wish was to come to Oregon, so we did, and he enjoyed his life here for three years. Then he died.

Shortly after that, with no thought of marrying again, I met a man at a singles' dance. In 1995, he became my third husband.

My husband John is Portland's oldest firefighter; he is still working. He is a big man, over 6 feet 5 inches tall, and I am 5 foot 2. We are the funniest-looking couple on the dance floor.

My life has not always been pleasant, but it has never been dull. It's been either extremely wonderful or extremely terrible.

Why did you decide to write a **Dear Mom** *letter?*

My college degree is in English literature, and I always said my second work would be writing. In fact, I'm working on a novel now. When the opportunity to write this letter arose, I really wanted to do it, and it turned out to be a therapeutic experience. I got to tell my mother things I had been holding in my heart for years.

Were there any surprises for you when you were writing your **Dear Mom** *letter?*

(*A noticeable pause.*) The surprise was how relieved I felt after I had written the letter. I really didn't expect that.

The other thing was not exactly a surprise. When you're growing up, you think your life is normal. But as I worked on the letter, I had a growing awareness that our life was not so normal—and that I had a truly amazing mother.

How would you describe yourself now?

I'm really happy and contented. This is the best part of my life, now, in my late 60s. I have someone who loves me, who brings me flowers. I have a great romance. Every decade of my life has had its own particular joys and sorrows, but the one I'm currently enjoying is the best of all.

Has your mother influenced you in the way you are a mother?

Yes, my mother influenced me very much. She created

the person she wanted me to be, and I'm still trying to live up to her expectations.

I feel that my mother tried to give me all that she dreamed and wanted for herself and never had. My own goal was for my children to have a peaceful, secure home. I wanted it to be a safe haven for them, and I think it was. They had good childhoods.

What do you consider to be your biggest successes and accomplishments?

I don't feel like I've succeeded or accomplished anything important. I do feel that I've never lived up to my potential.

On the personal level, maybe my role as surrogate mother to some very special people would count as an accomplishment. I went out of my way to help them, and it made a difference in my own life.

Professionally I don't feel like I accomplished yet what I'm supposed to. Maybe it will happen with my novel. I'm still trying.

What about your son?

Yes, my son. I have a wonderful son and I am so proud of him. I don't feel like I deserve a lot of credit for him turning out the way he has. I tried to give him a good life. In some ways I didn't live up to what I thought I should have been for him. I think sometimes children turn out well in spite of their parents, not because of them.

Your biggest disappointments or regrets?

Losing my daughter, of course. Losing my mother. Just this awful sense of loss. Once you've lost your family, you can't find home again. It's gone and there's no way to get back to it. You're always waiting for the other shoe to drop.

I'm disappointed that my relationship with my father was so difficult. It wasn't all bad. We used to sing together and I loved that part. My father had an abusive father who ruined him as a little child. He was a custodian in the school system. He was very bright; he could have done better than he did, but he seemed to have a fear of success that kept him back.

Throughout my life I've tried to be a good Christian. I have a really strong faith in God that keeps me going. When my daughter died, my faith underwent the supreme test.

At a time like that, you don't fake faith. Either you have it or you don't.

Fortunately, I had it.

Still do.

Rosemary Mayo

often dreams of her best friend—her "mum." But even with great love, there still can be regrets.

• • •

Dear Mum,

So many false starts—and I thought this was going to be easy! All I want to tell you is—I'm sorry.

You know that I love you; you know that I miss you still; that sometimes I feel you right there next to me. I'm usually driving alone when that happens, which makes sense; you loved your "runs"!

But did you know that sometimes I resented what I thought of as my "loss of freedom:" Sometimes I wanted to go out without you; sometimes I wanted to take the boys to the beach or the pool and stay there all day, and I was angry that I had to take you home.

When I was a child, you were my best friend, more fun than any of my other friends. No one would play "the bad guy" more willingly than you; no one built better hideouts; no one would lie in a hot stuffy tent all afternoon without complaint. So why couldn't you see that I wanted to do the same for my children?

But why didn't I tell you instead of harboring resentment? Because I was angry with you for getting old. You weren't supposed to age or become sick.

When I dream of you (which is often), you're never old; you're frozen in your middle years, when I would have been about 20 or so. Remember how we'd meet in the city for the day? We'd dress to the nines, eat at a fancy restaurant, browse the expensive stores, and end up at the flicks to see an old John Wayne or Victor Mature!

I wanted you to stay like that forever. And if you had to get old, I wanted you to do it quietly, so I wouldn't notice. How could I have imagined for a moment that you would sit contentedly in blankets, knitting like a sweet old lady? You were never a sweet old lady! You didn't even like old ladies. You were spunky, funny, demanding, generous, cantankerous, loving. And you, too, were angry at your old age and ill health. You did not go gently into that good night.

I wish I'd said, "Sorry."

I had the chance. Your last night in the hospital. You took my hand as I was leaving and asked me if you were going to die. You never spoke of death—far too un-British! So I should have known you were afraid that night. I should have stayed—we could have talked. But I brushed it off. "Don't be silly," I said. Oh Lily, I'd do anything to change that night.

You never spoke to me again. I held you the next morning and begged you to tell me you could hear me, just once. But it was too late.

So now I'll say it: I'm so sorry.

I hope you can hear me.

PROFILE: Rosemary Mayo

Rosemary's eyes grab my attention; they are large, intense and very clear. She is tall and slender, and looks much younger than her 57 years. She has a lot of energy and still speaks with the clipped accent of her native England. Rosemary writes fiction and teaches community college students and jail inmates the skills they need to pass the high school equivalency test.

Tell me about your work and your family.

I work as a writer and a teacher. My four sons are all grown. And I've been married to the same man for 35 years. That's something! *(She smiles.)*

Why did you decide to write a **Dear Mom** *letter?*

Well, I think when you told me about it, it just seemed like such an incredible opportunity to talk to my mother.

Were there any surprises for you when you were writing your **Dear Mom** *letter?*

No real surprises, just clarifications, I think. Why one feels guilty about things: Guilt piles up, and this forces you to sit down and think, "Why did I feel guilty? What was I guilty of?" *(She stops here, and then returns to the question a bit later.)*

I guess there was one surprise—okay, it just flashed through my head. The surprise was the realization that I was angry—finding out that I was angry because she was old. My mum wasn't supposed to get old.

How would you describe yourself now?

Pretty lucky, happy.

I've had a good life.

Has your mother influenced you in the way you are a mother?

Well, one thing, she never ever hit me, never laid a finger on me, and I don't know if it's because of that, but I vowed I wouldn't hit my children. And I didn't.

She also became a friend to me, not just my mother. And with my kids, I wanted to be a lot of fun as a mother. And that was entirely due to her, because she was a lot of fun.

She was not afraid to say "I love you," and we've passed that on. Our kids say "I love you" on the phone in front of people.

Your mother had a legacy of love?

Absolutely! She loved a lot.

What do you consider to be your biggest successes and accomplishments?

(*This question makes her smile.*) This takes some thinking; this is difficult. Having a good life, having a fun life, I think. I'm not a big work person, really. I just have a very ordinary little job, but I've been fortunate enough to have a happy life. *Great* husband.

Your biggest disappointments or regrets?
I honestly don't think I have any. Nothing that's important.

Grace Lee

credits her mother for being ahead of her time. Yet it's never easy for mothers to strike a delicate balance— protecting their daughters without putting an iron lid on their emerging sexuality.

• • •

Dear Mama,

I awoke one morning several years after your death and said aloud, "I forgive you, Mama, for all your mistakes. Please forgive me for mine." I wasn't specific. I must have been dreaming about some transgression between us.

Most of our skirmishes were benign, and I blazed no major individual trails. But no mother-daughter kinship is without the struggle of growth. Mothers try to mold their children, who put up the necessary resistance. Our history was like most people: a balancing act of good news and bad.

In most ways, I was lucky. You loved your children with a fierce quiet. I know you thought that a passionate display of emotion was tacky. Emigrating from Russia in 1899 while in your mid-20s, dignity was the only thing you owned. Or maybe that was your nature. Hard to tell. Though you may not have hugged me to your bosom with bursts of emotion, you touched me with loving hands, and I felt safe. I never doubted my value.

You told me when I was a small child that a famous doctor had treated you successfully for a tipped uterus before I was born. He then advised you to become pregnant. You said, "I decided to have a baby, and your birth made me well." Now that was a terrific thing for a child to hear.

You were a contemporary person for those times. For someone born in the 1890s, you had an amazingly modern psychological awareness. The summer I was 10, you took me for a walk in a small forest. It was more than a friendly stroll. You commented that I had developed breasts quite suddenly, and that this was a sign of an approaching event. You told me that my body was preparing for me to experience menstruation. You told me that menstruation was natural and that I mustn't be frightened by the sight of blood. You compared it to the leaves that fall from the trees in autumn. "When you are married and ready for a baby, you will get pregnant and will not menstruate for nine months. Menstrual blood will go to your baby who will grow in your stomach." You didn't explain how the baby would get there. And I didn't ask. I was too awed with the new intimacy coupled with the stunning news about my body. Three months later I menstruated. How dear of you to have so gently prepared me. How sensible to give me vital facts without the weight of sexual information.

But what was dear at 10 was a millstone in my later youth. You were like almost all mothers of your generation. Daughters were taught that we had one first-class prize—virginity. Someday we would reward an eligible man, who would certainly expect his wife to be inexperienced in the ways of sex. To challenge this in the 1940s was unthinkable. I accepted this inevitably. You were proud of my reputation as a prude.

I was so compliant. My role in the family constellation was "good girl." You were always a little surprised when I asserted myself. I remember when I was 15 and cigarettes called my name. I wanted you to give me my first cigarette. You offered to quit smoking if I would not start. Even in the 1940s, we knew that this habit was a health hazard. I rejected your offer, because I knew the few cigarettes you smoked were important to you. You never were the victim of nervous smoking. Three a day was your limit. With your morning coffee, after dinner, and before bedtime. When you realized that I was going to smoke anyway but I didn't want to sneak them, you relented. You did give me my first cigarette. Unfortunately, when I lit up, there was instant pleasure instead of choking. You then extracted a promise: that I would smoke only those that I would enjoy thoroughly. I promised—and kept it for several years. There was peace during my teen years.

The year I turned 20, World War II began. We were living in a modest place in Florida, hiding from the Chicago wind and snow. Your clever elder son, our family's main breadwinner, had sent us there for the winter. He was movie star handsome, charming and afflicted with a bit of a character disorder. Yes he was, Mama. He was also generous and fun loving, and we all adored him. All character disorders get adored, and he was no exception. But I'll bet he never untipped anything for you when he was born. He didn't have to. He just had to *be*. I idolized him too—until that winter, when I found out he was no Prince Valiant.

The prodigal son came to visit us for a week or two. The two of you decided that you needed to tell me that the woman who managed the apartment house was someone I should not socialize with, because she had had sex with my brother on the beach one night. You repeated that story to me after he left.

I was furious. It was our first real confrontation. The apartment house manager was an attractive, smart woman of substance who supported her 11-year-old twins.

I suppose this incident gave me a warning that even women of quality were diminished by casual sex. How dare my brother gossip about a casual dalliance. I was sure the occasion was not sacred to her, but it was too incidental to him. That should put his own character in doubt.

I told you that it was my brother who was the slut. You didn't argue the point with me. We both knew that, slut or no, the American male was royalty. But I had so admired your wisdom and fair play until that day. You weren't perfect after all.

You must have known that there was no danger that I would indulge my natural impulses. Until marriage, daughters of my era had a proscribed path. They followed it as chaste as possible. We ignored simmering volcanoes.

If one had the means for college tuition in those years, the standing joke was that it was a good place to earn a "Mrs." degree. I would have enjoyed a serious academic pursuit, but there was no tuition money. You assured me I was obviously intelligent and well-read. Pretty, to boot. I would attract a plum (a good catch). But I wasn't looking for a plum, just a perfect mate. Anyway, we needed my salary, from doing whatever, to help put bread on the table, despite my brother's major contribution. I didn't have the energy to pursue formal education after a 9-to-5 job—or the ambition to rise in the corporate world. So I worked in the human misery business of social services, where one needed academic credentials to have a full-blown career.

I was very angry with you during those years. It wasn't clear to me until many years later that my anger was displaced. I was upset with myself. I had not been able to mobilize the needed stamina to inch myself toward authentic goals. It was simply easier to accept the status quo and smolder than to stoke a fire. Not your fault, Mama. Nor mine, either. We did the best we could under the circumstances we found ourselves.

I learned endurance from you. I learned tenacity from you. I learned pride bordering on arrogance. All of which saved my sanity when my husband and my only child died. I mobilized myself to accept reality without screaming. Too bad. I paid a high price for a display of bravado learned at your knee. I had been carefully taught that a stoic demeanor was vital. It was unbecoming to display grief. I bled inside instead.

You were already in the throes of Alzheimer's disease by the time I received my B.A. at 40. You were no longer living by the time I got my master's degree at 50. I don't think it would have thrilled you anyway. You would have preferred my having another family that would love me and care for me. Mama, you did not have a fairy wish. That's what most people think of as a shelter. I don't recommend it for others but I have carried my own umbrella through the storms of life for over 40 years. I tried to make them productive and even enjoyable times. What other choice?

Mama, you taught me how to stretch a dollar—but not how to save one. So I am the only person I know who doesn't own his or her own home. But you are not to blame. I saw others invest their money while I was spending it. It was my responsibility to develop the fiscal sense you did not teach me. Given your background and philosophy, it is reasonable you might have thought money sense was déclassé for women.

I realize that had you not been a product of your time, there might have been other avenues that would have added purpose to your life. You were very bright, albeit undeveloped. But in those days, feminists hardly existed. Between Harriet Beecher Stowe and Golda Meir, there are few models.

You had an ironic sense of humor, so necessary for living through the storms of life. I share this with you.

Mine is more ridiculous than yours. You claimed my humor embarrassed you on occasion, but I think you enjoyed me at my most outrageous.

When you began to fail, we didn't understand your condition. I was often impatient with the signs of your aging. Sometimes I showed it. No child wants to admit her parent is becoming fragile. I was no exception. Had I not been burdened beyond endurance, my connection with you during your waning years may have been more patient. All my emotional energies were focused on struggling through college while trying to rearrange my life. Mere survival was a trial for me then. I think you understood this. You loved me unconditionally.

I try not to use "coulda, shoulda, woulda" in my life. I wasn't as devoted to you as circumstances warranted. It's a regret. Toward the end, you didn't have what I would call a life worth living, and I waited for you to find the comfort of death.

When you did die, I was shocked that I felt shock. After losing my child and a young husband, I expected calm acceptance. Death at your age is the penalty nature extracts for being born. No one is exempt. Yet your leaving my life in any condition left a unique hollow. Now more than 30 years later, I actually don't miss you. But I remember you with love, mercy, and gratitude.

I realize that your only son had to be your favorite, and my emotionally needy sister claimed most of your attention. Still, I felt you liked and respected me most— and that was more important than love, somehow.

Profile: Grace Lee

I've read Grace Lee's book, *On the Way to Over the Hill: A Guide to Aging Gracefully* (1997, Educare Press). Its wit and hard-won wisdom make me eager to meet her.

I am waiting for her at the restaurant when I see a gray-haired lady approaching the door. She has bright eyes, a great smile, and carries a cane. "I only need it sometimes," she tells me, folding it up.

Tell me about your work and your family.

I was born in Chicago, the youngest of three children. We lived for a few years in the city. Then we moved to Downers Grove, a suburb.

My father had a shoe store. Both my parents were Russian Jews. I had a mostly nonreligious upbringing. We did acknowledge some holidays. My father would talk about the history of events. Passover, for example, was celebrated without rituals but an annual retelling of the dramatic story of the Diaspora. And he closed the store on the High Holy Days.

When I was growing up, women weren't expected to have a career; in fact, it was almost taboo. I graduated from high school but I didn't go to college. Girls didn't go to college. I worked as a secretary.

When I was 21, our family moved from Chicago to California. I spent seven years in the San Francisco Bay area. The rest of the time, I was in Southern California.

I waited a long time to get married. I wanted someone bright, amusing, and fun. When I was 28, I met him: Laurie. We were married for seven years.

When I was 35, I lost my child and my husband in the same year. First my son died; he had Tay-Sachs disease. He was almost 4 years old. Just 10 months later, my husband died of a sudden heart attack. He was only 35.

Either you survive such losses or you don't. However, I was not interested in getting married again. I couldn't survive another loss. But I didn't join a convent. *(She smiles broadly.)*

After my son and my husband died, I went to college. I'm very proud that I went to college at the age of 35.

Professionally, I tell people I was in the human misery business.

In my life I've had four careers: as a secretary for social service agencies, a social worker, a community health worker, and now I'm a writer.

Why did you decide to write a Dear Mom letter?
You asked me and offered me money. That was a good reason! *(She laughs.)*

Were there any surprises for you when you were writing your Dear Mom letter?
No. I'm very in touch with myself. I knew what was there, and I see parts of myself in my mother and father.

How would you describe yourself now?

I'm adorable. *(She laughs.)* I think I've always been a realist. I'm sturdy. I once said I was tough, but I'm not. Sometimes I'm self-indulgent. I buy strawberries if I want them. I don't own my own home, but I've had some luxuries!

Time is yours to spend; you don't want to waste your time. If I don't want to write, I don't have to. I'm not bound to do that.

I've had a long life. It's been filled with lots of stuff. Everybody's got something. About 25 years ago, I had a double mastectomy for breast cancer and also part of my lung removed.

Did your mother influence you in the way you were a mother?

My mother was just thrilled that my child was born in the 1950s. When I was little, parents were told to have an ironclad schedule for feeding. And people were suddenly aware of germs. I encouraged my mother to kiss her grandson as much as she liked. And he fed whenever. She accepted that style of childrearing with delight. My mother never criticized my upbringing of my child.

She was very modern and psychologically oriented. She wasn't demonstrative, but she was proud. She had very high standards. I knew she loved us a lot.

What do you consider to be your biggest successes and accomplishments?

I was going to say writing, because it's published. But there's more: I went back to college when I was 35—a freshman! It was hard, but I did it. When my college diploma came through the mail, I threw it against the wall. There was small pleasure in the process of getting it. I was well-read when I entered the hallowed halls. Certainly, the university added to my store of information, but my real goal was an entrée to a professional life. And of course, the pursuit of the diploma kept my life stable. Although it was also hard, I'm more proud of the master's degree I earned at 50.

Maybe survival is my biggest accomplishment. *(Another smile.)* At least that's what people say to me.

Your biggest disappointments or regrets?

Not having a family. That's every day, that's all pervasive. I was born to be a housefrau and a mother.

Irene Svete

marveled at her mother's fortitude, but sometimes wished she'd act more "like a mother"—and less like a lawyer. Only after her mom died did Irene learn some essential truths.

• • •

Dear Mother,

Over New Year's weekend, the *Financial Times* ran an interview with Thor Heyerdahl that made me think of you. The interviewer asked the 86-year-old anthropologist and explorer what kept him going. "Pure curiosity," Heyerdahl replied. "Every year I seem to find more and more interesting things to do and to learn about."

I suspect you might have said the same thing. When your vision began to fail, you discovered books on tape. When your feet made it impossible to venture far from home, you took up backyard bird watching. For you, living and learning seemed to be synonyms.

For the past six weeks, I've been working on this letter. Starting. Stopping. Ripping up what I wrote and sometimes writing the same thing over again. I've jotted notes on my office calendar. I've scrawled pages in my journal.

"This should be easy," I'd mutter. "Just write a simple letter."

After all, you and I spent more than half my life corresponding by mail, a chain of words strung like tatting from Ohio to Washington and back again. You sent me postcards from China, New Zealand, and Kenya. I replied with images of California, Oregon, and New Mexico.

Over the miles, we shared the details of our daily lives. We wrote about weather and books, election results and movies. A description of Friday night dinner with your friends Helen and Lib drew back sketches from my Sunday morning hike on Mount Si. You despised Nixon and Reagan, adored histories by Barbara Tuchman, and, despite turning 79, successfully navigated the often slick sidewalk leading from your law office to your Buick three days a week.

Looking back, I realize there *was* one subject we didn't write about—our feelings for each other. Oh, we signed our letters, "Love," and we said, "I love you" just before we hung up on our weekly phone calls. But we did not talk about our complicated, sometimes adversarial relationship. For years, the whole topic was too fraught with anger and confusion.

Mother, I admired you, even bragged about you to my friends. But for most of my life, I wasn't sure that what tied us to each other was really love. I never doubted Dad's love. He was easy to read, warm, with hugs a dozen times a day and a swat on the bottom when I really stepped over the line. Balding and nearly 50 when I was born, he seemed perpetually delighted by the idea of fatherhood. Even his teasing told me clearly that I was his daughter, a long-hoped-for and totally unexpected offspring, and I was wonderful. His death at 58 guaranteed that he would never lose his hero status in my heart. You, however, couldn't be frozen in time.

With Dad gone, everyone expected you to update your teaching certificate and return to the classroom. Instead, you chose to enroll in law school. A 47-year-old single mother, you even won over the torts professor who belittled the handful of women enrollees by addressing the class as "gentlemen" because no lady would enter the practice of law.

Family legend has it that when the Legal Aid Society wanted to rent Dad's old law office suite, you told them that you came with the equipment. If they wanted the office, they would have to hire you as their legal intern. What was it like to work in their office all day, then drive 25 miles into the city and sit in a classroom for three hours, and then get up the next morning and do it again? To do it three nights a week for four solid years?

No one ever seemed to match your stamina and fierce pragmatism in the face of crisis. When my first husband threatened to throw my clothes on the front lawn and set fire to them, you ordered me to grab a neighbor and a camera so I would have proof.

"Don't act like my lawyer," I wailed into the phone. "Act like my mother."

But your mothering style was never cookies and sympathetic outbursts. You were cool and cerebral. After

Dad died, I felt like a plant—fed, watered, and turned toward the sun—but otherwise pretty much ignored.

Do you remember our trip to Alaska in 1986? When we were three days up the Inland Passage, I kept trying to rehash those losses with you. I was deep into therapy. But you just wanted a vacation.

I kept trying to tell you what it meant to be 10 years old and left so much on my own after losing my father and then his parents. We had lost a person a year from 1963 until 1970. You had a doctorate in coping with loss. You had buried a father, a husband, and both his parents. Two of your brothers-in-law were dead: one from cancer, another from a heart attack. A third was paralyzed by a stroke. You had suffered a miscarriage two years after I was born and helped nurse a sister-in-law through breast cancer less than a year after her husband died.

Our cabin on the cruise ship to Alaska was pale blue and windowless. We lay stretched out on the berths. I had been talking for a long time, pouring out two decades of anger, resentments, and grief. You rolled onto your side and began putting on your shoes.

"I was devastated when your father died," you said, in the same precise tone you used in the courtroom to state the facts of a client's case. "I did the best I could. I'm going out on deck now. You're welcome to join me."

That was it. No excuses, no apologies. I could let go, step out into the air, and enjoy the wonders in front of me—or I could continue to sit in that windowless room and stew about the past. I put on a sweatshirt and went outside. We leaned on the rail for almost an hour watching for whales, not really talking—just being together.

Today, on my desk at home, I keep two pictures of you. The first one from 1930 shows a gangly Appalachian farm girl and her two cousins, the three of you astride a plow horse. You are all wrapped in winter coats, and the horse is still in harness. In the other photo, taken in the 1980s, you are riding a camel on the volcanic slopes of Lanzarote in the Canary Islands. Your hair is gray, but your hazel eyes are sharp, and your smile is almost the same as that farm girl's.

I never heard you express a single regret for chances missed or things left undone, not even when you knew you were dying. Even today, I still marvel at your ability to sidestep the should-have-dones and might-have-beens that seem to ambush me in my own middle years.

I suppose it's your silence on matters of the heart that makes me treasure the journal I found while cleaning out your apartment. I nearly missed it. The hot pink cover of the steno pad tricked me into thinking it might be part of someone's case file. But there it was—the journal you started in 1981. The pages began like our letters—things you saw and did. I almost set it aside, but then it started to unfold like a peony in spring. You wrote of the man who brought a giddy teenage joy back into your life. You talked about your search for spiritual meaning. And most amazing, you talked about me. You detailed your trips to visit me, the places we had gone together, and my first stumbling attempts to carve out work as a writer. "I admire her verve, her outlook on life," you wrote. And for the first time, I read how much you missed me. Funny, the things we confide to our journals instead of each other.

Last March I celebrated my forty-fifth birthday in Paris. As I walked through the square behind Notre Dame early in the morning, I noticed the bulbs beginning to break through. The air was cold; the sky clear. An old man in a blue beret was feeding sparrows from the palm of his hand. I stopped at a postcard vender's display. I knelt there with my hands full of images—the Eiffel Tower at sunset, Lévy-Dhurmer's painting of Medusa, Napoleon's tomb—places and things I knew you would enjoy.

At that moment, I thought of the one line I would write if I could send you just one more note:

I miss you, too.

• • •

PROFILE: Irene Svete

I meet Irene at a small café on the campus where she works. She has short hair, a young face for her 45 years, and a great smile. Her energy fills the chair where she is sitting, and spills over.

She takes a lot of time on some of the questions, mulling them over, working her lips around the answers.

Tell me about your work and your family.

This is my second marriage, and I have no kids.

I was an only child. My father died when I was 10. At the time, my mother was 47. I currently work as a writer and editor.

I haven't always had the same work. I spent years trying different things. I've tended bar, worked as a telephone operator, driven a forklift, and sold Christmas trees. My bachelor's degree is in history and political science. I was a prelaw major.

When I was 20, I got married and quit college. Four years later, I went back to school and got my degree. I had my acceptance into law school—the University of Michigan—but I didn't go. I didn't want to get stuck in one place geographically. I had started writing in my last year in college, and I decided to make that leap. Eventually, I ended up as a newspaper reporter.

Why did you decide to write a **Dear Mom** *letter?*

Good question. I have no clue, to be perfectly honest. *(She laughs.)*

I liked the concept of what you were doing. I started doing a lot of what I guess you'd call self-archaeology when I went from writing hard news to fiction and essays. I had just completed a lengthy project in which I dug around in my own life. This seemed like the next step, to write a letter.

Were there any surprises for you when you were writing your **Dear Mom** *letter?*

Some. I was surprised at how much I did miss her. We weren't close emotionally, not in the traditional sense anyway.

My mother was 79 when she died in 1997. It was four days after I started my first job here on campus. I got a call around 5 a.m., telling me that my mother had had a heart attack. She was living in a retirement community and still working, three days a week. She had her own law practice, with a partner.

There had been some signs that her health was slipping. She had had breast cancer in her 60s, but she recovered. She had colon cancer in her 70s. That led her to buy the apartment in a retirement center, three years earlier. She liked it there. It was a good place, run by Quakers, with lots of consensus.

When the doctor called me on that Wednesday morning, I had trouble pinning him down on her condition. I'd just left the newspaper where I'd spent seven years, mostly as a police and courts reporter, and I wasn't sure what would happen if I just took off from my new job. I finally asked the doctor what he would do if it were his mother. He said he would come as soon as possible. I caught a red-eye flight that night.

She was alive and awake when I got there in the morning. That night, the cardiologist came in and said my mother had three clots in her arteries, and her kidneys were shutting down. All we could do was wait and see if they would begin working again on their own. We sat and watched the Cleveland Indians game. My mom was a hardcore Indians fan and the team looked good going into the playoffs.

The next day, it became clear that her kidneys were not refiring. The doctor said we had 24–72 hours before she died. She didn't say much. When the doctor left, she told me: "Go back to my apartment, and bring back my will and the rest of the papers so I can go over them with you." By the time I got back, she was drifting.

I stayed with her for a couple of hours, and then went back to her place to sleep. I woke up about 3:30 a.m., made a cup of coffee, and turned on the TV. I was channel surfing and stumbled onto an MTV video of the band Smashing Pumpkins.

It suddenly occurred to me I was almost the same age my mother had been when she took me to see Jim Morrison and the Doors in Cleveland, in 1968. I flashed on how my friend Kathy and I camped outside on the pavement all afternoon, along with tons of other people, waiting to get into the auditorium. (It was festival seating.) My mother was going to law school a few blocks away, so she spent the afternoon in the law library. Every couple of hours, she would wade into the crowd and check on us, then go back to studying.

That morning was the first time I'd thought of the Doors concert in years. Taking us to that concert, going so far out of her normal environment that way, struck me as such an amazing gift.

A few minutes later, the phone rang, and a nurse said, "You better get in here if you want to see your mother." She died that morning.

How would you describe yourself now?
I have no clue. It always changes day to day.
Healthy.

Do you feel good about your life?
I think so. The older I get, the more risks I take. I just—(*she seems puzzled*) I really don't know how to answer that question. I tell friends that I became a reporter because it's so much easier to write about other people.

I'd say I'm more content with myself now than I was in my teens and 20s. I don't feel I have to prove myself. I feel more settled in my own voice.

Who I am is just fine.

That was an issue between you and your mother?
That was a big issue. Not because she was a conformist. She felt uncomfortable with my approach to life, the instability of it—feeling my way, trying different things. When I was young, I always felt she would have been happier if I had picked one path and stuck with it.

I was surprised to learn from reading her journal that my mother admired my adventures. I spent many years thinking nothing I did would gain her approval. What I saw as disappointment I think now had more to do with her fears that I'd get hurt.

Has your mother influenced you in that you chose not to be a mother?

Good question. Possibly. Just maybe.

But I think it's more complicated. I don't think you can draw a direct line between my mother and that decision.

When I was younger, I believed you couldn't have it all without someone getting the short straw. Later, I began to think maybe you could, but there just didn't seem to be a right time. My mother gave me such a sense of life being more than home and kids. I was always afraid that I would miss out on something, so I kept putting it off. In the end, I had too crowded a life for parenting to fit in.

What do you consider to be your biggest successes and accomplishments?

(Irene takes time to ponder this.) Being able to make a living doing something I love. Having work that is a part of my life but isn't my whole life, work that allows me to have room for friends, enjoy the outdoors, and travel. Having a balance. That's probably more significant than any awards or anything along those lines, although I have those too.

Being a decent human being is an accomplishment. Being a good friend, participating in the community.

Your biggest disappointments or regrets?

I don't really have any regrets; I learned that from my mother. I'm disappointed that my first marriage didn't work out, but I don't regret making that marriage.

That is something my mother taught me—to do as much as you can with what you're given. Regretting just wastes time and energy.

But there was that five acres on the island I should have bought!

Joyce

struggles with painful questions about the choices her mother made more than half a century ago. Why, Joyce wonders, did her mother choose another man over her own husband and children?

• • •

Dear Mother,

I just phoned you to wish you Happy Birthday, your ninety-second. Since you are a frail 87 pounds, I worry about you. My family feels concern for you too. My children and grandchildren have positive feelings toward you, not knowing some of the things that took place years ago under the influence of the man you preferred to my father.

I cherish the memories of you before and after your relationship with this man, Roger, who had such an evil influence on you.

I haven't told my children and grandchildren about the agonizing events that still trouble me, more than 50 years later. I don't mean to cause you distress at this time in your life, but I wonder if you realize how much your leaving home for a man whom we disliked affected my brothers and sister and me as well as Dad and your parents: Grandma and Grandpa.

Our family—you, Dad, Jim, Will, Ann, and I—lived with Grandma and Grandpa. Thanks to Grandpa's financing, you and Dad ran the local grocery store. You spent most of your time there while Dad painted houses and did some general handyman work in our community. Those were happy years for all of us. Although you weren't home full-time, you were usually available four blocks away at the store. We children didn't really notice your absence. Grandma and Grandpa relished the activity of a full household, and we thrived under their attention.

Then World War II came. You closed the store, and Dad started working at the local war production plant. You left home to take a job out of town, leaving your four children (ranging from 2 to 14) in the care of Grandma.

At first it was fun having you come home on weekends. You helped Grandma fix big dinners, you brought home presents, and Dad beamed. Remember, he would sing "When Irish Eyes Are Smiling" and "My Wild Irish Rose" in his tenor voice. When I hear Irish tenors, I think of those days. Dad's Irish eyes were smiling then.

Soon though, it was obvious something was wrong. I remember being awake after you and Dad went to bed and hearing him whisper, "But you're my wife." Then, later, a woman who worked with you told Dad that you were very friendly with a man named Roger. After we all were in bed, I heard Dad sneer, "You and Roger in the moonlight." I didn't fully understand the implications of those words at the time, but I felt the tension between you and Dad.

During the week, life went smoothly. Grandma washed and ironed our clothes, made our meals, reminded us to practice our music lessons, scolded us when we misbehaved, and smiled when we brought home good report cards. What fondness we held for her!

You were Grandma's only child, and she doted on you. She was cheerful when you first left, but as time went by, she complained about your absence, questioning why it seemed necessary to you. As the situation with Roger became apparent, even Grandpa became grumpy. Dad no longer spent evenings at home playing checkers or listening to the radio with us children, but went to the village tavern instead.

When I was in high school, you took me to your apartment in the city. I met Roger. How I disliked him! He was loud and boastful. Yet when you were with him, you displayed a nonchalant joy I'd never seen. Confused, and wanting to please you, I tried to hide my aversion to him. I feared that you would marry him.

The war went on. I was now helping Grandma with the housework. Jim (my oldest brother) had joined the Air Force. You took a job as a medical secretary in a bigger, more distant city, and moved into an apartment with Roger. Meanwhile, Dad often didn't come home from the local bar until after we were in bed. Waiting for him, I would lie awake, terrified that he might have an accident or not come home at all.

My family knows you married Roger after you divorced Dad, and they know Dad drank. But I've never told them that Roger and you had a relationship long before the divorce, and that Dad's drinking began when you took up with Roger.

Despite your absence, Ann was an honor student. She was also on the drill team and involved in the school newspaper. But Will, at that time 14, was a problem. With his friends, he smoked and drank. On your rare visits, Grandma and Grandpa discussed Will with you. Your response was to blame Dad. At the time, I, in my adolescent mind, blamed Roger for Dad's drinking and for Will's behavior. My reasoning was simple: Had you been home with us instead of away with Roger, Dad wouldn't have started drinking, and Will, who adored you, would have had you and Dad to guide him. Six years ago, when Will died, I wondered if he would have lived longer had you been home during his teen years.

Dad continued to live at Grandma's with us children until you formally divorced him. After he left, he moved in with his two brothers. He no longer drank. He stayed with my family several times before we moved out of state. He seldom talked about you, although he once commented that one thing you could never take from him was his children.

When Grandma and Grandpa finally met Roger, they were not impressed. Grandma told me that though Dad had his faults, he was far superior to Roger. Roger shouted at Will, telling him he was "good for nothing."

He presumed to tell Grandpa how to manage his property. He alienated Jim, interfering in Jim's business, accusing him of overcharging and disparaging Jim's ability to customers. Soon Jim and his wife stopped communicating with you. They did not visit Grandma and Grandpa if you and Roger were there.

Shortly after Grandpa died, your relationship with the family deteriorated even more. Grandpa had taken great pride in having a piece of property in his estate for each of us grandchildren. When neighbors asked him why he had bought another piece of land although he no longer farmed or logged, he responded that land was a good investment to leave his grandchildren. He made it clear, however, that you were to have the house. He wanted to be sure you had "a roof over your head in your old age." Then Jim learned that you and Roger managed to change your parents' will, cutting out the gifts to the grandchildren. Grandpa had already given Jim the summer cottage, but Jim was dismayed that we other children would not get the gifts Grandma and Grandpa had meant for us. Will, Ann, and I agreed that we didn't want to upset Grandma with legal action, nor did we want to make your behavior public. But Will's family was now totally alienated from you.

Over the years, Roger's influence over you had no limit. When you and Roger moved into Grandma's house, you mistreated her. Unaware that she no longer had control of her estate, she insisted that she was mistress of the house. So you locked her in her bedroom.

Grandma climbed out of the window to get help from the neighbors. She asked Jim to help her move to the local assisted-living home rather than stay with Roger and you. I never asked her whether she had discovered that you and Roger had obtained her Power of Attorney. Like Ann and me, she loved you so much that she did not want to recognize the appalling acts Roger had instigated. And of course, I do not want my children to know about your abusive treatment of her.

Grandma lived to be 96. Ann and I flew her out to visit us during her last years. Jim and Will often had her stay with them. Grandma enjoyed her last years. Time was good to her.

Time wasn't as kind to you and Roger. He had several strokes and was in a wheelchair for several years before he died. By then, you had only the house left. Grandpa had been wise, knowing you would need it.

Now, you are here, living in an apartment near Ann and me. I'm glad you are nearby for us to share our children and grandchildren with you. Although you are still estranged from my brothers' families, we love you and take joy in your well-being.

Yet Dad, Grandma, Grandpa, and the rest of us suffered so much heartache when you let Roger dominate your life.

I wonder if, over the years, you have regretted losing part of your family because of Roger.

Was he worth it?

Profile: Joyce

Joyce meets me at the hotel where I am staying. It is almost lunchtime, but after learning I had a late breakfast, she too is not hungry. We sit in the lobby to do the interview. Joyce is dressed like a lady, in a peach dress, with neat hair and small, tasteful jewelry. She seems nervous as we talk.

Tell me about your work and your family.

I'm 72 years old. I have five children. They all live nearby. For a while, they had a new baby every year. We have 11 grandchildren.

My husband and I have been married 50 years. We're still very much a happy couple. *(She smiles.)* When my youngest was in kindergarten, I began teaching, working part-time in community colleges.

Why did you decide to write a Dear Mom *letter?*

My sister Ann and my brother Jim and I have talked about Mother's life and the heartache she caused her parents and us. Jim thought it would make an interesting story. Jim's family is completely out of touch with our mother—they refuse to communicate with her. Ann and I tried to get them to reconcile, but it didn't work.

My sister and I feel differently from my brother; I think it's because we're women and tend to emphasize family. Also, I remember my mother being loving and protective when we were little. Ann is the baby of the

145 ·

family, and so she was too young to be aware of the years when Mother left us.

Were there any surprises for you when you were writing your letter?

Yes. It was probably good for me to examine the past in words, yet it felt painful instead of cathartic. I wished that I hadn't started it.

While working on the letter, I was surprised that the past still bothered me so much. Writing about what happened brought back those painful feelings. I was uncomfortable realizing I was not totally rid of them.

When Mother first left us, I was deeply hurt. Then as the years went by, I was angry. I no longer feel that way. My mother is old and frail, and I regret that my brother has not forgiven her. Ann and I have taken responsibility for caring for her.

Mothers are important no matter what their behavior. I know how important I am to my children.

How would you describe yourself now?

Kind of humdrum. A retired teacher who does her volunteer work. I work with a children's organization, I serve on committees, sing in the church choir, and I am very family-oriented. We all get together once a month when we celebrate the birthdays. I do appreciate my grandchildren. They're still young enough to think I'm great. They beam when I compliment them!

Has your mother influenced you in the way you are a mother?

Well, I don't know that *she* has influenced me. My grandmother was the one who supported, disciplined, and cared for us.

Maybe my mother influenced me in what to avoid, such as not being there for your children. I certainly would never break up my family for another man.

Indeed—I did do something that I hadn't given much thought to before—I praised my husband to our children. As they were growing up, I pointed out their father's good qualities and gave him due credit. I wanted them to appreciate him, and they do. It is wonderful to see.

What do you consider to be your biggest successes and accomplishments?

Probably raising my children to be good people.

Your biggest disappointments or regrets?

(*She pauses and thinks about this awhile.*) I can't really think of any serious regrets.

Suzanne

wrestles with her desire to know more about the birth mother she lost.

• • •

Dear Mom,

If you are still alive and your memory is well, I'm sure you must remember me. We were together for only a year, but now I am a mother too, and I know there are moments and images that time won't erase, even though that time was so short and very long ago.

I cannot remember you. Maybe there are small fragments scattered here and there that are part of that vague sense of familiar that suddenly swarms through a present moment and leaves me struggling to find the memory link, but those will never yield a true memory.

I do have a photograph. It shows you and my father standing in front of a car, my father with dark wavy hair and a confident smile, you with lighter hair and squinting your eyes against the sun. You look just like me, and I am always squinting in outdoor photos. I also have a letter, but it's not from you. It's from your sister. She begs my foster parents not to go through with the adoption. She explains that you are really a good person who made a terrible mistake. It doesn't say what the mistake was, but my adopted mother says you wrote bad checks, mostly to buy small things, like baby clothes, for other people. For that, you went to jail. The punishment seems harsh. So does losing all your children.

I guess you must have learned that my adoptive mother worked at the same school as your sister-in-law. Since the adoption came about from a personal connection, much more than usual was known about why I was given away. Over time, my new parents told me that information.

I know that when you went to jail, my father filed for divorce. Before you had finished your sentence, the court awarded custody of all three of the children to him—even though he had to put all of us into foster care because he traveled for his job, and even though he decided that I would be better off adopted out. It seems a great punishment for such a small crime. Perhaps you were able to reconnect with the others because my father kept them—but you never saw me again.

I wonder sometimes if you think about me when there are television stories about reunions of separated birth families. I watch, and sometimes I think maybe I should try to meet you, or my biological sisters and brothers. But fear always overcomes my curiosity. First the fear that too much will be expected of me (it's hard enough to keep up with all the relationships already in my life), and then the fear that I will be rejected.

When I was a teenager, I had the opportunity to attend a wedding where I could see my sister and my brother without having to reveal who I was. I didn't want to go. I didn't want to know. I didn't want to step into the world of that black-and-white photograph of you and my father and the old car. The photograph was the only image I had of the world that was my past, and it always seemed surreal and very frightening, as though I am really someone else, and if I open that door—if I discover everything about that other family, that other life—I won't be able to put it back in the box.

My adoptive sister went through a service to discover her birth mother, and a stepbrother as well. She was welcomed with open arms, and they did not expect too much. Maybe I will find you, my birth mother, too, but so far I always end up deciding I can think about it later. I put the unknown back in the attic trunk of my mind, far away from daily thoughts.

In the media, there are never stories about those of us who chose to leave the past undisturbed. So I always have a vague sense of guilt as I shrink away in fear from what others passionately desire. I wonder why I cannot be like those other people; I think they must be "normal," and I am not.

Maybe I know too much. Maybe the little I know about you makes me afraid to know the rest. We look alike. We share a trait. You are a writer, published in magazines, I understand. So am I. I began writing at an early age, reading my stories out loud to the class, and writing plays we would all perform. As an adult, writing is still my strong suit, although I seem to keep more ambitious goals for this talent in the same attic box, with "LATER" stamped on its lid.

I wonder if you would just as soon stay in this box, or do you ever wish a letter would come that begins like this one? Finding you would not be difficult—not technically, anyway. I have the address of a birth cousin. She lives in a town near my own. I think most of my birth family lives in the same city as I do—maybe I have even met them. Sometimes strangers come up and think I am someone else they know, because I am such a look-alike.

If a chance encounter were to open this doorway, I would not have to decide. Fate would open the door from the other side, and whatever is there would come through to me. I would not have to walk past the gargoyles surrounding the door, menacing me with their fiery eyes, horns, and tridents.

One time, a man told my daughter that she looked just like a woman about the age of—and with the same name as—one of my biological sisters. But we could never discover who this mysterious look-alike was, because the man had only met her in passing at a fitness club, and he never saw her again. It seems odd that a resemblance would be so strong that a third party would connect her to a stranger. I think that mysterious look-alike must have been my sister, and I hoped for a while that this man would see her again, and my daughter could inquire.

Once in a great while, I see someone who looks a little like me, and I wonder. I understand that you remarried and had a second family, so I have half-siblings as well. They say we are all connected by six degrees anyway: What are the odds that an acquaintance of mine knows someone in my birth family? Perhaps I do.

If we were to meet, I'm not sure what I would say. I guess I would tell you that my adoptive family had a lot of problems too, and I always felt a little out of place, but I would not trade the outcome. I am okay. My life is good. I have two daughters, and we count each other as great blessings in our lives.

I cannot imagine what you must have gone through in losing all your children. Your parents probably told you that they came to see me a few times after the adoption. I didn't know who they were at the time, but years later my mother told me they were my grandparents. By then I could only vaguely remember what they looked like, but I did remember a pleasant older couple who were always so delighted to see me and were much more attentive than other visitors. It must have been difficult for them too. I guess you know they wanted to adopt me too, but the judge ruled in favor of my foster parents.

I would also like to tell you that I hope your life has been good. I like to think that you learned from your mistakes and went on to find new happiness with your second family. I wonder if you ever told them about me.

I was told that you moved to another city and worked for a while as a photographer. I have a good eye for the camera too, and although I have never pursued it, I have always thought I might one day.

Mostly, I am drawn to anything creative, and I have a hard time staying interested in anything that is not. I think we are probably alike in that way. I have always thought we are probably a lot alike, and I often wonder if that has been sort of a barrier in giving myself permission to devote more time to my interest in writing. Perhaps I worry that if I let myself become more active in this endeavor, I will become you. I will start out writing fictional stories, and end up writing fictional checks.

It isn't very logical, but then most of our fears aren't. Perhaps it is nothing more than the fear of being swept away from reality by my own imagination. That happens, of course, when I write, but I always seem to find my way back.

Perhaps I fear that if I work on something long enough, and hard enough, I won't return. I will be pulled through the celluloid of that old black-and-white photo back to my natural gene pool. Unchecked by the constraints of my uncreative adoptive family, these genes will spin out of control and I will become the crazy creative they say you were. That would certainly explain all my unfinished work. Of course, it is also possible that my talent is best suited to shorter pieces, the sort of things you wrote.

I guess I might try to tell you something about what it was like to be adopted. I would have to tell you that I never liked the label of "adopted child." My adoptive parents went way out of their way to tell my sister and me how special we were because they chose us, and I knew they meant well, but I always wished they wouldn't. I didn't want to be special; I wanted to be normal.

The kids in my neighborhood all seemed to know, and they would occasionally ask if I didn't want to find my "real" mother. They, of course, could not imagine not knowing their parents, so they had great curiosity and slight pity that I did not. I hated being different, and I especially didn't want anyone to feel sorry for me. Sometimes adults would do the same thing, in a different way: "Oh, you seem so happy now. I remember when your folks first adopted you, you were the saddest little thing!" I always felt exposed, unmasked in front of others as an imposter. *Adopted child;* not *real child.* Rescued from darkness and brought into light.

As I grew older, I learned to avoid this stigma by keeping my early past a secret, but I never really got over the feeling that adoption lacked the legitimacy of natural birthright. Every time I fill out a health questionnaire and I have to write "unknown" on the questions about family medical history, I feel exposed as an "irregular" once again. I wish I could tell you that I have pulled this weed out of my garden by this point in my life (it seems like I should have), but the roots are very deep.

If we were to meet, I wonder what you would want to say to me. If you are like me, you would mostly want to apologize and explain. You would want to be understood and forgiven. I don't know if I would understand, but I might.

I do know I would tell you that you have always had my forgiveness.

I hope you were able to give the same to yourself.

• • •

PROFILE: Suzanne

Suzanne meets me at the hotel where I am staying. She has an easy manner and talks with energy and insight. Suzanne has been incredibly busy at her job, and one of the first things she tells me is how she misses having time to write.

"I'm not happy with the idea of not doing creative writing," she says as we walk to a restaurant for breakfast. "I've always been a writer. In fifth grade, I had my own publishing company. Kids liked my stories!"

When she lived in the Midwest, Suzanne contributed articles to a local newspaper and edited the newsletter for the Women's Political Caucus. "At that time, believe it or not, in that town, you couldn't get your own library card if you were a woman, married, and not working!" We discuss this amazing-to-me fact for a little while. Then we go back to talking about writing.

"My birth mother was a writer of fictitious checks, and my fear of creativity is irrational," Suzanne tells me.

As an adult, Suzanne has participated in writing workshops. "It totally blew me away that people found my work so funny and engaging. Humor is easier for me to write than other kinds of things. I think of it as a parlor trick, an easy fallback from the more serious thing I would rather achieve."

Tell me about your work and your family.

I'm 57 years old. I work for the state government. I've been married to my second husband for 25 years. When we got married, he had four kids, and I had two.

I grew up in a suburb—it was actually a pretty rural area then, but it's a suburb now. We had a half-acre of land.

I was adopted when I was a year old. My adoptive parents were well-meaning but inept. We were worlds apart. They were focused on things—and on appearances. They were very uncreative and unimaginative.

My adoptive mother was "inside the box," with good intentions, but no antennae to feelings.

My adoptive father was an alcoholic. He would get upset because I lost things. My head would be somewhere else. My father called me "Dumbo," because he knew I was smart, so I had no excuse for losing things.

I have a lot of painful memories about my childhood. However, on balance, I have to credit my adoptive family for a lot because I think I turned out pretty okay. I know they loved me, even though they had a hard time understanding me. It's probably not that different from a biological relationship.

After high school, I went to college and worked for the government. First I was a secretary, and then I became an administrator. I had two daughters. They are now adults, married, and both living in the area. Also I have one granddaughter and two grandsons.

I never went back and got my degree. Economically I didn't need it. I thought it would be nice, but it didn't make sense money wise.

I quit my job in 1986, and I was gone for almost 12 years. During that time, I had a small business, and then my husband and I moved to a more rural area for two years.

But I really like living in a city. I never thought I would be a city girl, but I like the diversity.

Why did you decide to write a Dear Mom letter?

I found it cathartic to write this letter to my biological mother. I wasn't sure what I wanted to say. It goes to the issue of secrets—and intrigues the writer in me. It can be therapeutic to get it out. Things you hold inside can imprison you.

Everything I said I had never before put in writing. It felt liberating. It didn't seem nearly as terrible on paper—actually it felt good.

Were there any surprises for you when you were writing your Dear Mom letter?

Little surprises, maybe.

I think I understood the circumstances of my adoption and how the identity of my natural mother affected my life. Even though I had no relationship with her. Until I wrote about it, I didn't see how she affected my life, because I never tried to explain it.

I don't know if she's alive. I haven't made contact. I could—I do have names, right at my fingertips. But I've never been able to make a decision to do it. It bothers me that so many people want to make contact, but I don't. There are reasons to do it—medical history, for one.

As I wrote about my biological mother, I tried to figure out why I couldn't contact her. And when I finished the letter it seemed possible that I could. I'll just have to think about it.

When I was 18, my natural aunt said there was a family wedding. She told my adoptive mom. I ran out in the yard and cried. I felt that my adoptive mom and my aunt were treating me like a product, but I'm sure they didn't mean it that way. I didn't want to deal with being adopted. I always felt like I had a stigma. It was like saying I had to be someone else, to have two identities: one to please them, and one to preserve my own self-worth. It seemed callous to me.

My natural aunt and my adoptive mother, who knew each other, didn't know that being adopted was like a bomb for me.

My aunt used to come out and visit me, but I didn't know she was my natural aunt. Then she moved, and I never saw her after that.

I remember her daughter (my cousin) had legs that looked just like mine. I had no idea we were related, but it struck me. Later, I remembered that my aunt and my adoptive mom had showed me photos of my sister—but I didn't know she was my sister.

I do look exactly like my natural mother. I have a photograph of her, and I'm a dead ringer for her.

How would you describe yourself now?

I'm lucky. I'm happy with my life. But there are still some weeds in my garden. This issue, with my natural mother, is the big weed in my garden.

Has your mother influenced you in the way you are a mother?

Growing up, I felt like an alien from another planet. I didn't feel safe. I didn't want that for my kids.

Mostly I tried not to make the same mistakes. I didn't emulate anything. My adoptive mom was always concerned about appearances. You know how kids will blurt things out. I would tell them something funny, and my parents would get mad at me. We had lots of secrets when I was growing up.

So as a parent, I tried not to be that way. I encouraged my children to be open, to be who they are. I wanted them to feel accepted.

What do you consider to be your biggest successes and accomplishments?

I think probably having my two daughters. I don't think there's anything more important. They care about the world, about themselves. We have respect and love for each other.

It wouldn't matter what else I'd done—no accomplishment or task can measure the legacy you pass on to your kids. That's a way of making the world a better place. I think I've done a pretty good job, not perfect.

Your biggest disappointments or regrets?

That I haven't been able to spend more time writing. It's a pretty solitary pursuit; as I get older, I like the solitude. And I regret the barriers I haven't been able to get past.

Awareness is the beginning of change. I think my *Dear Mom* letter helped me pinpoint the obstacles; maybe it will help me get past them.

It's all getting past the fear that my real self is dangerous, because my mother was creative and a little crazy, I think.

Jane Mozena

recalls sharing laughter with her mother during her wonderful early childhood. But one year, things changed fast, as her mother spiraled downward into an agony of mental illness.

• • •

Dear Mom,

We never talked about what we left behind in Walla Walla, Washington.

Just before we moved to Walla Walla, when I was three, you and I posed for a picture in our yard, in Jeffersonville, Indiana. You're sitting on a wooden park bench in the picture, your arm around me while I stand on the bench, my arm around your neck. You're wearing a white sundress that flows around you down over the bench, and open-toed white pumps. Your black hair, streaked with gray, is swept up and back from your face. My dark hair is in a pixie cut, and it shines like my black patent leather shoes. You've got me wearing a dress white like yours, with a Peter Pan collar and puffy sleeves. We're both looking off to the left, and smiling.

A week later, in an endless drive across the country in our tan 1947 Dodge, we moved to Walla Walla.

It was hot the day we drove by the sign for Walla Walla, on the edge of a flat dirt field that stretched forever. A tractor in the distance stirred a small dust storm around itself.

"Walla Walla," Daddy said. "The town so nice they named it twice."

"Walla Walla," I said too, and then said it again. I loved saying that town's name. I still do.

Soon we were in the town, driving along streets shaded by branches of tall leafy trees with fat trunks. We turned onto a street with more of those trees and two-story old wooden houses on both sides. Daddy turned the car into the driveway of one of those houses, a big white one. "Here we are," Daddy said. "Our house." Our house had a big front porch with a porch swing on the left side. I ran to that swing, jumped on the yellow flowered cushion and rocked forward, then back, then side to side. You had to urge me to get off and come in to see our new house.

You must have been happy during those early months in Walla Walla. You must have been happy, or I'd never remember those days the way I do: warm, vivid—one of the happiest times of my life.

You and I liked to laugh about the kittens. My best friend Kenny and I, and the other neighborhood kids, found the kittens in a garage by the alley. For some reason, we thought their being in a box in the garage meant the kittens were for everybody, so we each took one, named them for how they looked, like "Stripey," and "Gray-ey," put them in our pockets, and then ran down the sidewalk with the tiny kitten heads poking up out of our pockets. You saw us through our dining room window, then walked out the front door laughing, and called to us. You walked us back down the alley to the neighbor's garage, trying to be stern, but unable to stop laughing, then gently told us to put the kittens back. They mewed up at us from the box with their light blue eyes as we said goodbye, and then we ran back, kicking up dust in the alley.

It wasn't long after the kittens that I got a cat of my own, "Boots." Boots was no kitten, he was big, and black and white—and beautiful. You and Daddy walked with me to a house where we got him, and I got to carry Boots home. I was scared for a minute, because I thought he was growling and didn't like me. You and Daddy laughed, and you taught me about purring, and then I knew Boots liked me. I was proud walking between you and Daddy, carrying my very own cat down the street to our house.

When the sun finally went down on those long summer days, you sat beside me on my bed and read me stories. My favorite was "The Cow in the Silo," about the cow that was stuck in the silo and saved by being rubbed with shortening so she could slip through the silo door. Even though you read that story to me countless times, you always read it like it was the first time, like it was the most exciting story you'd ever seen. When the cow looked out the silo door with its huge worried eyes and mooed a moo that took up a whole line on the page, you read each "oo" of that "moooooooooooo...." You never rushed through it. No one could have read that cow-in-the-silo story the way you did.

In the fall, those big trees on our street dropped mountains of leaves that my friends and I used to make forts and to jump on. Then came Halloween, and we had a Halloween party for all the neighbors.

That house in Walla Walla was the only house we ever owned, and that Halloween party was the only time we ever had people over.

You put shiny red apples in the gray metal washtub full of water. When you called everyone over to bob for those apples, you found each apple had a bite taken out of it. Everyone laughed, and you laughed the hardest. No one admitted being the apple biter, but I've always liked to think it was me.

Winter brought taller-than-me snowdrifts, and the Christmas tree. That was the Christmas I'd just turned 4 and got the black rocking horse with curly black hair all over its body and a shiny black mane that I braided. That was the Christmas I realized I was supposed to give presents too, not just get them, so I wrapped things around the house as presents. I gave you the green plaid beanbag ashtray, and you unwrapped it and thanked me, and you and Daddy laughed.

One night after the snow had melted, I was riding on my horse in the living room—when I heard you and Daddy yelling at each other in the kitchen.

"Keep your feet on the ground," Daddy yelled. I don't remember what you said back. Daddy said that to you many other times after that. "Keep your feet on the ground."

I have another picture of the two of us, taken at the beginning of that next summer in Walla Walla. In this picture, you are wearing a blouse over a print skirt. You look straight toward the camera, but your eyes don't look in the camera. Your hair is almost totally gray now and cut with bangs, straight, just above your shoulders. At your side, I wear a sleeveless sundress, and my knees bow out like I'm jumping up and down. My mouth is open, my face turned up toward you. I remind myself of a monkey in this picture, jumping up and down, squealing with my mouth open, trying to get you to look at me. Your face shows no expression.

It was dusty hot again in Walla Walla the afternoon you called me into the house, then into your room, the sun orange through the closed window shades, dust floating in the rays. You sat on the bed while I stood before you, and you cried and hugged me.

You told me men were coming to take you away, and that you didn't want to go. I wrapped my arms around your neck and looked in the dresser mirror at your back and my face, and my brown eyes were big. My hand patted your back. I wanted so much to save you, but what could I do to stop these men? I don't remember the men coming—maybe I was at Kenny's when they came—but by nightfall you were gone.

That night Daddy tied my shoes as I sat on my bed. The last rays of sun streamed in red behind him. A tear rolled down the side of Daddy's big nose. Daddy told me you had gone to the hospital because you were mentally ill, and that there was nothing wrong with that.

When I saw the neighbors the next day, I told them all that you went to the hospital because you were mentally ill. I repeated to them what Daddy said, that there was nothing wrong with that.

"Of course, Dear," they said, and smiled down at me. And I realized there was something terribly wrong—or else why would we need to say there wasn't?

Kenny's mom took care of me during the day while you were gone. One morning, Kenny and I were playing in his front yard when a long truck rumbled by, then squeaked to a stop in front of our house. Two men opened big metal doors at the back of the truck, and then laid down a brown metal ramp with a crash. A few minutes later they came out of our house carrying the velvety dark green sofa and chair that you and Daddy had bought at the furniture store when we moved in.

One Saturday, Daddy took me on a long drive to see you at Eastern State Hospital in Medical Lake. We turned into a long driveway and drove past many big brick buildings, and then parked near the one Daddy said you were in, the one furthest from the road. We rode up an elevator, and walked down a shiny yellow floor, to the end of the hall.

You walked out into the hall wearing a cream-colored smock over a black skirt. I thought you looked beautiful, and I thought you were going to have a baby. But you said "No." You said it was from the insulin shock treatments they gave you. The men dragged you out of your house, took you far away to the giant brick hospital, and made you fat.

It seemed to me like you were gone for months, though it may have been weeks. But I know it wasn't long after you came home, when summer was ending, that we left Walla Walla. I didn't understand we were leaving until Daddy put Boots into a wooden crate one morning and told me he was taking Boots back to the people where we got him. Daddy said we were moving to an apartment in Eugene, and Boots couldn't live there. Other things couldn't come to the apartment either. They went into storage, including my horse.

Two years later, when we moved to a house in Portland, I got my horse back. I was excited when Daddy went to get it, but when he carried it through the door, it wasn't the same as in Walla Walla. I was too big, and too old.

It was hard to live with you those years after Walla Walla. While your illness took you further and further away from me, I kept trying to get your attention, like in that picture of us in Walla Walla where I am jumping up and down.

Sometimes I felt sad for you, like the time in third grade when you were our Blue Bird leader for only one day and they said they didn't need you anymore. I was mad at the people who hurt you that day, and I was mad at Donna from school for telling me our house looked like I rode my bicycle through it.

Mostly I was mad at you. A lot. I was mad at you for embarrassing me when you walked to Safeway in your filmy white nightgown and robe with the fuzz around the neck and sleeves, wearing those gold high-heeled slippers you insisted were dress-up shoes. I was mad at you for standing up at the PTA meeting to complain that the Russians were poisoning the school lunches. I was especially mad at you for chasing my friends out the front door, through our yard to the street. You yelled behind them that they had hurt me, when nothing had been going on that could possibly have given you that idea. I was mad about our filthy house with your urine pools on the floor, globs of your hair on the sofa, all the dishes dirty with cigarette butts smashed into them.

For most of my life, I was mad at you about those things. And sad for me that I had to grow up this way with you.

On New Year's Eve, when I was 15, you were in the kitchen looking out the window toward the backyard and the downtown Portland lights. You talked softly to yourself, rocking back and forth on your heels. You wore that loose lime-green housedress you wore all the time those days, and it was covered with coffee and food stains. Your gray hair streamed wildly down your back to your waist. You smelled like sweat, rancid grease, urine, and cigarettes. Outside, fireworks popped, bells rang, pots banged, the city celebrating the arrival of 1963. Inside, in our kitchen, I screamed at you.

"Listen to me!" I screamed. "Look at yourself!"

I screamed louder. "You're filthy. You stink!"

You kept rocking, whispering to yourself.

"Daddy's going to leave completely if you don't snap out of it." Daddy came home every few days that year, brought groceries, put them away, and left again.

I felt bad for screaming at you. I said I was sorry. "I'm just trying to get through to you," I added, more softly, crying. "Because I love you."

You didn't say anything to me. You kept talking to yourself—smirking, laughing, and rocking.

I got mad again and screamed at you some more.

I hated you a lot of the time those days. Then I'd feel guilty for hating you, and write in my diary about how much I loved you, how I wished I could get through to you, how I wanted so much to help you.

But now, all these years later, I look at pictures of you when you were young and beautiful in Virginia, a William and Mary coed, a leading lady in community theater plays, and I feel so very sad for you, for how your life turned out. When you sat on the sand with Daddy at Virginia Beach, the stunning couple in the middle of a large group picture, you looked toward the camera, radiant, confident. I feel sad knowing that you never would have dreamed that day how your life would turn out, how your brain would turn on you. "Paranoid schiz- ophrenic" was how they said your brain turned on you.

When I look at you and Daddy so happy together on the beach, when I read the letters you and he wrote to each other whenever you were apart during the years before Walla Walla ("Darling," the letters begin, or "Dearest"), I know you never could have imagined how the two of you would end up after Walla Walla.

When I graduated from high school, Daddy had you committed again, this time to Dammasch Hospital. Then he divorced you. After that hospitalization, you were better for a number of years, and I am grateful for those years.

I am especially grateful for your joy in being a grandmother. Paul and Claire loved the way you cooked poached eggs on toast for them, always just right, never too hard or too runny like mine. And they loved the way you sliced watermelon, holding the long knife in the air, and then yelling "hi-yah!" as you brought the knife down and sliced the melon in two with one blow.

But you never were the same as you were when we first moved to Walla Walla. You were never the same girl with the "eloquent eyes" described in your high school yearbook, the confident young woman on the sand at Virginia Beach, the young mother laughing about the kittens and the bitten apples at the Halloween Party. And my heart breaks for that loss, for our family, and especially for you.

When we drove out of Walla Walla, past the dusty fields for the last time, we left behind much more than Boots. We left the dreams for our family in Walla Walla, although we would continue to live together for many years.

I hope that what we wish for after death is true, that you are in a wonderful place now, that you are the smiling girl again from Norfolk and Virginia Beach, and that I will get to know that girl, that we will run and laugh together on the beach, when my time comes.

• • •

Profile: Jane Mozena

Jane is a dark-haired, lively, attractive 52-year-old woman. Her energy is infectious; at certain points during our conversation she almost bubbles. Jane smiles often but turns solemn when she talks about troubled times.

Tell me about your work and your family.
I was a social worker for about 15 years, and for much of the time I focused on developmentally disabled children and adults. Then I decided to take a break in 1991. I now work part-time as a bookkeeper for my husband's law firm. And I write.

Why did you decide to write a **Dear Mom** *letter?*
I thought it might be helpful. I had some things I wanted to say to my mother. I wish I had appreciated her more.

Were there any surprises for you when you were writing your **Dear Mom** *letter?*

Yes. I was surprised at how angry I still am at my dad, for abandoning us.

When I was growing up, our house was a terrible mess, dirty and smelly. My father didn't clean it up. He had his own room in the house, which he kept meticulous.

But really, when I was in high school, he was living someplace else. He had a girlfriend. After my parents divorced, my father did pay my mother alimony.

I'm also mad because my parents had privileged upbringings. They both grew up in well-to-do families, they both went to good colleges back East. Yet when it was time for me to go to college, my father gave me double messages. He made fun of me for taking secretarial courses, but he told me he couldn't help me with college.

I'm angry with my father because I think he was selfish.

Just when I graduated from high school, he put my mother in the hospital. And it was his idea to put me in a hotel, the kind of hotel where I had to share a bathroom down the hall, not a great place. I can't imagine doing that to my daughter. He paid for a week; that was it. Then I stayed with friends, I got a job, I worked, I got married and divorced, and working as a secretary, I put myself through college.

How would you describe yourself now?

I am a *very lucky* person. *(Big smile.)* I have a wonderful husband, and we have two great kids. My husband supports and encourages me. I have nice writer friends. I even won a prize for my short story, "The Dissection" in the 1999 Clark College fiction contest.

I write a lot of short stories. The sad stories feature a girl named Ruthie. I also write happy stories about a middle-aged woman, Julie. Julie is like me now: She's having fun, and her life is good.

Has your mother influenced you in the way you are a mother?

Yes.

My big theme is being normal, looking normal. Because everyone, when I was growing up, knew my mother *wasn't* normal. She didn't stay home; she was out sometimes, acting crazy. No one reached out to me. Except one teacher. I was in the seventh or eighth grade, and he did approach me. But I wouldn't talk about it. My father always said, "Don't hang your dirty linen in public." There was such shame associated with her condition.

I know I laid that on my children. I had an expectation that they behave, that they not stand out, not draw attention to themselves in a negative way.

I did worry, as they got older, that my kids might have inherited something. I was particularly sensitive to any signs of difficulty.

Once, when I was working as a social worker, I was talking to someone and a colleague thought I was talking to myself. I laughed it off, but inside I was terribly upset that someone would think I was talking to myself. I didn't want anyone to think I was crazy.

My kids and my husband knew my mother was mentally ill, and they accepted her. They liked her. When my kids were young, there were several years when she was doing well. She was a good grandma, paying attention to my children. And during this time, she worked—as a telemarketer, a manager of an apartment building, and in a factory.

But then she started going downhill again. She had delusions. She was living in her own apartment, but she would yell at people. She left water running. Eventually, with the help of a social service agency, we got her to move to a retirement home. She was 88 when she died.

What do you consider to be your biggest successes and accomplishments?

I raised two nice children; they are good people. They both graduated from college.

Being married almost 27 years.

My work as a social worker, when I was able to make a difference, that's an accomplishment.

I quit smoking. *(She laughs.)*

I run, and a few years ago, I completed the Portland Marathon.

I've done writing I'm proud of.

I was a good daughter in a lot of ways. Basically I was there, when my mother needed something. I feel some guilt about all the resentment I have about my childhood. For the first four years of my life, my mother must have been a good mom, because I have such wonderful memories.

Your biggest disappointments or regrets?
Sometimes I think about the path I could have taken, writing from the beginning. But I got sidetracked. I accomplished some things as a social worker, but I also have regret that I didn't become a writer sooner.

If you had had the mother we all wish we had—do you ever think how you might be different?
I wonder if I would be more confident inside. Not always wondering if I look right, or worrying about not fitting in.
I like to think that I gave my own daughter that confidence.

Dear Mom

Women's letters of longing

Beth

reflects on a childhood etched with her mother's anger and depression, and struggles to accept her mother's decision not to try for a more fulfilling life.

• • •

Dear Mom,

It is so hard to write this letter. It feels like pulling a string, and a whole ball unrolls—and who knows what's in it? Dust, dirt, and pieces of broken glass. There is so much I never told you that I don't know where to begin.

I don't know if I ever felt close to you. I must have, when I was very little, but I can't remember the feeling. I do recall hugging you—and you hugging me back. It hurts to remember my arms around you and how soft you felt.

I know as a kid I drove you absolutely crazy. I asked questions—about sex, about everything!—and argued with your answers. I was relentless. I challenged your authority and power over me.

I didn't want to end up like you, and I was terrified, for a long time, that I would: that the poison, the contamination in our family, would get to me, like I thought it got to my brother. Something that stole hope, love, and freedom—and replaced it all with a stifling, deadening control. As a kid, I didn't know what to call this thick, gray fog: It was just "normal." With my abundance of energy and feeling, I was designated the "crazy one" in the family. Everyone—you, my father, and my brother—all agreed on that.

Sometime, I think during my teen years, I realized that the pervasive, suffocating negativity had a name: depression. Mom, I think you have been depressed for about as long as I've known you—most of the time, a low-grade depression that seeped into everything and robbed joy, passion, and pleasure from so much. I remember your anger so well, but now, looking back, I also can see how scared you were. How afraid to admit confusion, fear, loss, love—anything of feeling and of life.

Way down deep, I am still afraid that this toxicity will get me. I know that depression can run in families, that we are all affected by our biological inheritance. But Mom, why do you so steadfastly refuse to get help? Over the years you have totally resisted all attempts by me and by your doctor to persuade you to take medication, just to *try* and see if it can help. You are bound and determined to be the way you are. You do not *want* to change. After decades of struggle, I think I have reluctantly—painfully—come to accept this.

Maybe that's an overstatement. How well I accept the way you are seems to vary by geography. When I am separated by hundreds of miles, I accept your choices. I even have "perspective."

I can remember your slapping me—hard enough to leave marks on my 8-year-old face. Now, as an adult, I say to myself, "She was full of rage. She was overwhelmed. She didn't mean to do it."

I had refused to eat my breakfast, and that was just one more bit of obstinacy than you could stand. After you hit me, I ran into the bathroom and prayed to Peter Pan to come and rescue me. I can still see that little girl in the blue dress in the bathroom, looking at herself in the mirror, at the angry red marks on her face, and wishing so fiercely she could just disappear.

Now I am an adult, and I don't need Peter Pan to rescue me. I am okay. I have my own life, and it's mostly a very good one. Still, when I am in the same room with you, or even just in the same house, after only a little while, the air becomes toxic, and I can't breathe. I remember this so vividly, as a teenager: I had to get away, *I was suffocating.*

I decided fairly early that I had to look outside our family for what I needed. (And Lord knows, I made lots of mistakes in that quest.) But for years, I still wanted your approval and understanding. When I was 15, I wrote a poem about you:

> *My mother's room is where no one goes.*
> *Cool and bare, the walls do not speak,*
> *never greet the visitor*
> *who in the doorway stands*
> *young, wondering, how to get in?*
> *My mother is in there, hidden.*

I wanted to believe that you were in there, that you understood me, deep down, and that if only I could reach you, with the magic words, the magic signs, the magic *anything*, you would become the mother I so desperately wanted and needed. Someone who actually liked me the way I was, who didn't need to label me as "wrong," who didn't want to change me fundamentally.

That was my dream, and it took me years to realize that it was never going to happen.

But Mom, I don't want to be unfair. I need to give you some much-deserved credit. I know that you wanted the best for me—what you considered to be "the best." Intelligence was important to you. And you never—not once—demeaned my intelligence. Instead, you always told me I was very smart. And you praised my good grades and encouraged me to do well academically. So I grew up with a pretty strong faith in my own brain power—justified or not—and I don't think I realized what a gift you gave me until I was in my 30s.

Despite your emotional turmoil, you also provided me and my brother with a pretty stable life—something I took completely for granted as a kid. It must have been especially difficult for you, being depressed, to keep house, make meals, and go to PTA meetings—but you did all that. My brother and I never lacked for any necessities. We had extras too: art and music lessons and stints at summer camp. We learned to be responsible, work hard, and live by other basic values ("Read every day," "Pay your bills," and "Don't lie") from you and our father.

On my last visit, I could see you are becoming frail. It is hard for me to realize that. You don't seem to have rages anymore. Rather, a pervasive, all-encompassing anxiety has replaced your anger. You worry about finding the bathroom in a restaurant, about where I park the car, about a slight sniffle. Nothing is ever okay just the way it is: The food, the weather, the very air you breathe is faulty. You fret and fuss almost constantly.

But—you don't attack me anymore. Not even with words. We have very formal, polite, almost always exceedingly inconsequential conversations. I have learned not to question you about anything of substance, because you become irritated and change the subject. You don't ask much about my life, and I oblige you by not even attempting to tell you anything intimate.

I don't know how much longer you will be alive. It pains me that you have had so little joy in your life.

I so wish that I could see you overwhelmed with happiness, if only for a short time. Steeped in pleasure from seeing your wonderful grandchildren, a sunset, whatever. I don't expect your joy to come from me; I gave that up a long time ago. But it would be so nice to see pure pleasure in your face, or to hear it in your voice.

It would make me feel really, really good.

PROFILE: Beth

Beth is a busy person who is juggling many obligations. After a couple of schedule changes, we finally manage to find a time that works. When we sit down together in her office, Beth concentrates on my questions and ignores a ringing telephone.

Tell me about your work and your family.

I work in public relations and development for a nonprofit agency. I like my job because there's a lot of variety: One minute I'm being interviewed for a radio program, the next I have to meet with the Board of Directors. In a single week I might talk to agency clients, potential donors, corporate boards, and so on.

I've been married for 25 years to my husband. And we have a daughter.

Why did you decide to write a **Dear Mom** *letter?*

Because I knew there was a lot there.

I don't think I've ever been able to talk, to *communicate*, with my mother. I've tried. She can't hear me. Maybe it's also true that we are so different, I can't hear her either.

For much of my life, my mother operated out of fear and anger, and that makes any kind of closeness very difficult.

When I was younger, I used to try to reach her. But I also went outside my family, to friends, for support, and

I think that's what saved me. My friends liked me, and they didn't think my energy, ambition, and enthusiasm were character flaws!

Over the years, I developed strong connections with several wonderful women a few years ahead of me; I pieced together bits of their nurturing and advice into a kind of patchwork quilt of mothering. These women have been great role models—they are accomplished and independent, and they also enjoy being moms.

Were there any surprises for you when you were writing your Dear Mom letter?

Yes. I realized that I needed to honor my mother for the things she did *right*, while bringing me up. She took good care of my physical well-being. I never wondered where my next meal was coming from, or whether I had toothpaste or clean clothes to wear. I took all that for granted, and I now know that it takes work: It doesn't just happen.

Also, she provided me with a structure, with middle-class expectations that have served me well. The skills that my mother taught and modeled for me enabled me to survive and get jobs when I left home.

Another surprise was uncomfortable for me, but it's true: I carry a biological and psychological legacy from my parents, a tendency to depression, negativity, a willingness to believe the worst instead of the best about people and situations. I'm aware of that, and I work to overcome it, still. I expect that I will be working on it for the rest of my life.

How would you describe yourself now?

I consider myself a *very* lucky person. I have a wonderful husband and daughter; I adore them both. I have true, close friends. I love my work, even though sometimes there is too much of it!

I have a full life; sometimes it is overwhelming. But I know how fortunate I am to be in this situation. My life has turned out better than I ever thought it would or could.

Has your mother influenced you in the way you are a mother?

Yes. I waited a long time to be a parent, because I wanted to be sure I would not repeat certain patterns.

I made a vow I would never hit my daughter. And I never have.

I also vowed I wouldn't yell at my child, but of course on occasion I have.

My mother also influenced me in very good ways: to provide structure, to be reliable and dependable to my child. My daughter knows she can count on me. She has that security, although right now she's a teenager, and she would sometimes like me to disappear!

What do you consider to be your biggest successes and accomplishments?

That I am a better person than I used to be.

I give people the benefit of the doubt more. I try to understand more and judge less.

I think I've been a pretty good mother to my daughter; she knows she is loved and cherished. Of course, my husband deserves a good share of the parenting credit: He is a great father.

I know my daughter is a wonderful person, but I hesitate to take all that much credit for it. God made her that way. The credit my husband and I can take is that we didn't screw her up. At least not a lot.

The other thing, I don't really know quite how to say this: My husband and my friends know I can be trusted. I am very loyal. That doesn't mean we don't have disagreements—we do—but the connection is solid. Over the years, I've learned to maintain close relationships, through the lows and the highs. These bonds help me feel centered, at home—even sometimes, at peace.

Your biggest disappointments or regrets?

That I can't eat anything I want and be thin. *(She laughs.)*

Seriously, that I'm not close to my mother or my brother, and I don't see any way that's going to change. I wish I could feel differently about them, but I don't. The best I can do is a polite, rather formal relationship in which I honor my obligations.

That is sad.

On a professional level, there are the usual "shoulda, woulda, coulda" regrets. I could have gotten my master's degree; there was a time when I really considered it, and my agency would have paid for part of it! But I had a small child, and it was just too much. I love my work, but it's not my whole life.

So I guess my regrets demonstrate just how fortunate I have been overall.

Claire

faces her mother's contrasting legacies: a love of justice and leadership—and a deep-seated fear of men, which fed the overweight that Claire is now finally managing to shed.

• • •

Dear Mom,

I have started this letter many times in my head and wondered what I would say to you on paper that I couldn't say in person. It's uncomfortable to know that I have a trunk full of feelings that I have not expressed over the years. Yet my life is full, I'm happily married to a man I love, we have a wonderful son, I have good close friends, and I am building my own successful business in my favorite city. So what possible complaint can I have about my mother?

I'm not sure I would call it a complaint, so much as a desire to talk with you in a way that doesn't seem possible in person. I don't remember having many talks with you, long or short, about how to solve problems— or how life works. You had your hands full, raising four other kids and keeping a controlling mother-in-law at bay.

I did watch you, and I learned a great deal. My most treasured values in life came from you: my sense of justice and compassion, my willingness to fight for what's right, and my penchant for organizing and volunteering for leadership positions in every group that I join.

But I also learned to be afraid. Afraid of intimacy, afraid of losing control, and afraid of pure joy! It's not that you didn't want me to be happy. On the contrary, you worked very hard to give me every opportunity. You always said, "I just want you to be happy" or "Whatever makes you happy is fine with me." But always woven into the conversation or situation was your mantra, "Be careful." In your desire to protect me, you made me doubt my own value.

In sixth grade there was a turning point for me. I had a huge crush on a neighbor boy. He and I had been spending time together and I thought he might ask me to "go steady" with him. I remember sitting in our car telling you about it and feeling excited that a boy really seemed to like me. You had a very concerned look on your face, and you asked me, "Honey, are you sure? I don't want you to get hurt." You also said something about how young I was, but the damage was done.

How could anyone really like me, especially a popular cute boy, who was a bit more dangerous than usual because he went to public school? Well, the boy never asked me to go steady, and I developed an insecurity around men that still haunts me today. That may sound silly coming from a woman who has been married for more than 25 years to the most wonderful man, but it's true.

I don't think this one incident would have had much impact had I not gotten the idea that boys—and later, men—were dangerous characters. I learned that by watching how you reacted toward my younger sister. As a little girl, she was the one who was always throwing her arms around men—uncles, grandfathers, and neighbors—or prancing around in a playfully suggestive manner, in the quite innocent way little girls often do. She always seemed to be getting in trouble because of what you considered to be her wayward actions. You were either glaring at her disapprovingly or grabbing her by the hand to stop her flirting. It was clear to me that there was something wrong with her because she generated that much attention, particularly from men.

So I played it safe. I was the good daughter. I was the nice one. I would stay out of trouble by attracting men with my sense of humor and my personality. And always lurking in the back of my brain was the feeling that I was second rate in the "sexy" department. But that was okay, because good Catholic girls were not supposed to be sexy!

I didn't fully understand it at the time, but the second part of the message was that men were not to be trusted. All they wanted was to take advantage of me—to have sex! So it was better if I didn't get too close. They would only break my heart or hurt me.

So fast-forward to today and my current struggle to become healthy. I've begun again to peel off the layers of fat. For the fourth, and I hope final, time in my adult life, I am losing weight and finding long lost feelings in the process. As I shed the pounds, I become more anxious, afraid that I might also lose my wonderful husband, and our relationship. It doesn't seem to make sense, but that's how I feel.

After all this time, I still don't completely trust that my husband really loves me. It's hard for me to see what he could possibly want from me beside sex. Because I have stayed hidden for so long, I'm not sure who I am underneath all of this fat and whether or not he would still want the "real" me. My other fear is that I may want someone else! I believe that I have stayed overweight for most of my life so that I can avoid these fears, so that I can cover up my feelings of love, lust, and joy. It's safer to stay fat than to risk being open and vulnerable.

I want to put all those unresolved feelings to rest so that I can keep the weight off, feel totally safe, and finally enjoy this wonderful life that my husband and I have created together.

Mom, thank you for all the spirit you helped create in me. It gives me the courage to press on and succeed in spite of my fears. I'm sorry that you grew up with a basic fear and distrust of men. I didn't realize how strongly you felt until I started listening more closely to how you talk about men and how you act around them. It surprises and saddens me that you hold on so tightly to that point of view.

But I am determined not to repeat the pattern. It stops here and now.

I love you.

Profile: Claire

When I first met Claire, she was bright, articulate, attractive—and very overweight. At the time of our interview about a year later, she had lost close to 50 pounds. She looked wonderful, and more importantly, she radiated positive energy, warmth, and intelligence. We met on a rainy February day to do her interview.

Tell me about your work and your family.

I'm currently building my own business in corporate public relations. I work with executives and their staff. I troubleshoot and help them with crisis communication.

I've had a sort of eclectic career: It certainly hasn't been linear.

After high school, I flunked out of my first semester of college. I moved back home for a few months. Then I took a job with a mortgage company as a file clerk. I worked for that company for nine years, working my way up to being a mortgage broker.

Then I met Phil. We dated for a while, and I knew he was the one!

I was 25 when I got married. Four years later, I quit the mortgage company. I got interested in painting and took some classes. Then I opened my own painting studio and held classes in my house.

I also got pregnant and had my only child, Daniel, in 1976. My husband and I were good parents. Phil has a wonderful way of putting himself in a kid's place and understanding how he would like to be treated. Daniel is now 25 years old, and he works for a computer company. I'm very proud of him; he's a good human being.

I never felt I would be as good a mom with more than one child. I was the oldest of five myself, and I remember fighting for time and attention. There were times I resented being part of such a large family.

When I took art classes, I realized that I really enjoyed going to school. I was a good technical painter, but not a great artist: I was a meat-and-potatoes artist.

At some point, I realized I needed a regular degree, so I decided to go back to college. I thought public relations and advertising would keep my interest. I loved school, and I graduated Phi Beta Kappa. It was overwhelming, because I had flunked out years ago, but to be acknowledged was so great. Aside from my wedding and having my son, I treasure my graduation and the Phi Beta Kappa honor.

Right around the time I graduated, we had to leave the city where we were living. It was a sticky, painful situation, involving business and family. So my husband got a job in Indianapolis, and we lived there for several years. I worked at several different office jobs and took care of my son.

Then my husband got transferred to California. That's where I got my first job in public relations. I started as a clerical worker, temporary and part-time, but I made myself indispensable, and within three years, I was a full-time manager with several big accounts.

I also did some consulting. I found out I could sell what I knew, and people told me I was really good at it. Plus, I enjoyed being my own boss. So a few years later, I opened my own business.

Why did you decide to write a **Dear Mom** *letter?*
Well, first of all, I thought the concept was interesting. And probably because my instinctive personal reaction was to resist and not do it. Anytime I'm avoiding something, it's a sign to break through it. I had so much energy about the topic—sort of like facing into the wind. I needed to do it.

Were there any surprises for you when you were writing your **Dear Mom** *letter?*
I expected a whole lot of anger and blame.

I was pleasantly surprised. I don't have a lot of anger—more sadness. I also realized that I'm not carrying around a lot of blame, and I'm glad about that. At my age of 53, it's a good time to write a letter, to reflect on this mother-daughter relationship. My mother did the best she could, but she could never be the perfect parent I expected as a child.

How would you describe yourself now?
I see myself as an emerging person. An unfinished work of art. Under construction. A work in progress. *(She smiles.)*

Has your mother influenced you in the way you are a mother?

I think so. *(With emphasis.)*

My mother said, "Be careful." That was her enduring mantra. The wonderful thing is that my husband gives me a reality check, because I'm a worrywart. *(Claire and I take a minute to laugh, as we share this quality.)*

My reaction now, when I feel fear, is to move *into* it, to deal with it. That's the opposite of what my mother would do.

I tried not to repeat the bad patterns in my childhood.

Growing up, I felt like I never had enough; money was a controlling thing, and food was a comfort, a measure of love. I didn't want Daniel to feel like that. I wasn't stingy with money—or with emotions—and I never forced my son to eat what he didn't like.

What do you consider to be your biggest successes and accomplishments?

Probably having a great marriage for so many years, coming up on 28.

Doing a good job as a parent: I often don't give myself credit for that. What the hell, I will! *(We agree on this. Why not?)*

Graduating from college—becoming an educated person.

Now I'm beginning to enjoy my success as a business-woman. I'm learning more about myself, my place in the world, and how to be a healthy, happy, sexual being.

That's amazing and wonderful for this baby-boomer woman!

I want to enjoy this wonderful life my husband and I have created.

Your biggest disappointments or regrets?

Maybe when I flunked out of college. I wasn't ready to go.

Probably the debacle of the business thing, the trouble between my husband and some relatives. It was very difficult; it took a long time to repair the relationships.

Nora

now treasures her mother's many gifts. But as a child, Nora longed for her mother's wide-ranging mind to focus more on her.

• • •

Dear Mom,

I am 5 years old and have just violated the "Don't bother Mom, she's writing" rule. I have opened the door to the upstairs room where you are working at a desk, and I'm running barefoot across the wooden floor to you when suddenly, my foot is impaled by a splinter. It's a brazen bid for attention, and it seems to have worked. Now my cries are real!

Thirty-six years later, I have stopped the theatrics, but I am still wondering: How can I stand in front of you and be seen?

Your world was always so big, and you gave your attention to so many things.

As a child, I resented this. In Massachusetts, still 5, I accompanied you unwillingly on a trip to visit Emily Dickinson's home. "Some day you'll appreciate this," you said when I whined about going. As a young adult, though, I was proud of you for your big world. When I told you my housemate was from northeast Spain, you asked if she was Catalan. Maria was astounded. "You don't know my mother," I told her.

But at the same time, your global outlook could be embarrassing. My teenage sisters and I would cringe at your unabashed ability to respond to the question, "Where are you from?" with the pronouncement, "I'm a citizen of the world!"

Although your world was big, it wasn't big enough to include attending a single one of my high school soccer games. I knew you didn't care for sports, so I never asked you to go. It didn't seem odd at the time. Now I watch my friends attending their daughters' games and wonder what it would have been like to have you there supporting me, rooting for me.

No, I couldn't stand in front of you with athletics. That didn't register on your radar screen. Academics, yes. Athletics, no.

So I played the academics card to the hilt. My 4.0s were the norm, and becoming valedictorian was a given. It didn't seem to matter that I didn't have a boyfriend in high school; that would come in time. Or so I thought.

I didn't count on the string of married men who sprinkled my romantic landscape after college. I never told you about that, Mom. That certainly didn't fit the program laid out for me. The program was: Ph.D.; husband—a fellow academic preferred, and definitely Christian; several talented and well-behaved children; and if I became an expert in my field, writing books and touring the country, glory be.

But my own path did match the unavailable love I learned at home. On the one hand, my forbidden liaisons all seemed so unreal. "It can't be me who is doing this." On the other, I was starved for love, so I would take the crumbs where I could, like some doomed noblewoman in a Victorian novel. I didn't tell you about those affiliations, because although in a twisted way they were triumphs ("Look, Mom, I'm loved!"), I'm not proud of them.

So I may have learned calculus, but I didn't learn to love and value myself.

It's not that you weren't loving when you were present. It's that I wasn't cherished. It's that I was a third child out of four, and you were a very busy woman. It's that I saw you not standing up to Dad's controlling ways and unpredictable outbursts. It's that I learned it wasn't safe to be me.

Yet if I sat on your lap when I was little, crying about something, you would hold me and say, "Bless your heart. You have such a sensitive heart." I knew by the way that you said it, that that was a good thing.

Mom, I never thanked you for demonstrating so perfectly how to savor a moment. Or how to tell a story with enthusiasm and drama, keeping listeners rapt. I never told you how I appreciate your ability to go to Plan B with no fuss when Plan A falls through. I never told you that I admire your "do-it-ness"—your ability to take on projects I find repulsive—like going through closets, drawers, and old boxes, sorting and throwing things out. I never told you how I envy your ability to sit down and concentrate on writing a poem, an article, or a book. The very skill that allowed you to tune me out as a child!

I never thanked you for teaching me to value and respect people and their struggles. When I was 13, I stood by you, puzzled, as a neighbor who had come over for tea and a chat burst into tears and cried in our dining room, seemingly for no reason. "She sees you and our home and looks at her own unhappy life—that's why she's crying," you later explained. "You'll understand in time."

Now, in my 40s, I am finally learning to stretch my empathy and compassion to include you. What must it have been like not to be treated as an equal of men in the academic world of the 1960s and 1970s, to have four children to raise, to be married to my crazy father, and to see no easy way ahead?

I'm learning to navigate our current relationship. I no longer get defensive and rush to correct your "inaccurate" perceptions of me. "That's my mom!" I think, with a smile.

I think I'm learning to love you as you are—the same gesture of grace that I wish from you! Each week brings me a new opportunity, when the phone rings, and I hear your voice, or when I call you. "*Nora!* Oh honey, it's *Nora!*" (All of this exclaimed to my father, loudly, as though I'm calling from China, or haven't been heard from in months.) "I'm in the kitchen, honey. Can you get on the other phone?"

Yup, that's my mom!

I love you, Mom.

PROFILE: Nora

Nora is a petite woman who looks much younger than her 42 years. She is neatly and conservatively dressed. We meet for lunch at a restaurant near her college. She focuses intently on my questions, and speaks carefully and thoughtfully.

Tell me about your work and your family.

I work as a college administrator, I'm single, and I have no children.

Why did you decide to write a **Dear Mom** *letter?*

I thought it would be interesting to see what would come up for me. In the process of doing the letter.

Anything else?

Often mother-daughter relationships are complex; that's certainly true for me, so I wanted to see what would be in there.

Were there any surprises for you when you were writing your **Dear Mom** *letter?*

I think it just made me more aware of my mother as a person in her own right, and what she went through in her life. It gave me a greater appreciation of her.

How would you describe yourself now?

I'm very interested in lots of topics; I'm a glutton for

learning new things. I would say that now I am very engaged in life. In fact as I grow older I'm trying to narrow my focuses and interests because I tend to get really scattered. I'm actually trying to concentrate on developing myself as a writer.

I'm also athletic. And very interested in people. And in observing people.

Do you feel good about your life right now?

Yes and no. I feel like I have a good life, but it could be better, so I'm working to improve those areas where it isn't as good as it could be.

Do you want to say anything more about that?

I don't think so.

Has your mother influenced you in the fact you are not a mother?

That's just the way it developed, that I'm not a mother. I would love to be a mother. I don't feel my mother has any bearing on my not being a mother. I love kids, and they love me. I volunteer on Sunday mornings at my church nursery. And I enjoy babysitting for my friends' kids. I've had people tell me I would make a great mother. That I'm not a mother is because of my father.

When you say it was your father...

It's because of his personality disorder: He was so distant and critical and not engaged in my life. And the relationship he and my mother had was so terrible, subconsciously I think I just decided I would never get married. So not getting married and not having a man in my life, I didn't have kids. I knew I didn't want to do the single parent thing. I thought that that would be too much, too hard. I would want to share parenting with someone.

What do you consider to be your biggest successes and accomplishments?

It probably would be the two years I spent in therapy, working through my stuff. It was probably the hardest thing I've ever done. It's not learning all the foreign languages I've learned, or getting all the academic degrees, or earning a brown belt in Judo. No, the toughest challenge I ever had was the two years I spent in therapy working through my issues.

It sounds like you think it was worth it?

(With great emphasis.) Definitely. Definitely!

Your biggest disappointments or regrets?

I guess I prefer not to look at my life in terms of regrets. It just seems like wasted energy.

Sally Flood

wasn't close to her aloof mother, but paradoxically this lack taught her the importance of paying close attention to her connections with her own children.

• • •

Dear Pebble,

All I can think about today is the Christmas of 1934. I feel depressed and close to crying.

We lived on Taylor Avenue then, in Seattle. We'd recently moved from Spokane. You and Dad had put everything in a moving van and rented a home on Queen Anne for the time being.

Our family was in turmoil. But I don't think I was aware of it then. I was only 9 years old. It was the middle of the Depression. Mary (my older brother David's wife) had come to live with us, bringing your first grandchild with her. Where was David? I don't remember him being there at all.

It was Christmas Eve. Dad wasn't home when all this happened. I don't know where he was. Maybe out getting presents for us.

You'd dressed up. I guess trying to make the night more festive. There was drinking, I'm sure. You and my older sister Betty got into an argument over the way Mary was taking care of the baby. Then it became a tussle, and you fell on the stairs, cutting your leg. I found you later, sitting in your room on a chair in the corner, your head in your hands, crying. I'm sure those tears were for much more than dirty diapers. The financial and personal mess Dad had created in Spokane caused you to lose your home and personal privacy. Plus your 13-year-old son was sick in bed with some undetermined illness.

My Christmas present that year was a doll with roller skates on. You got a cocktail shaker, chrome tray, and silver glasses. What a big deal. Every year at this time, I roll back those years in my mind. Through no fault of yours, they were the first of several difficult ones to come, most of which were tainted by alcohol.

I am writing this letter to you, because I am 74 now and grateful to know all the good things you left me. It took a long time to come to terms with who you were. Your private inside spaces usually kept me away from you.

But we had some lovely, smiling times together, didn't we?

Remember when you and I took the streetcar downtown and saw Kate Smith at the Orpheum Theatre? Another time, we saw Marion Anderson at the Music Hall. You and Aunt Dorothy and I saw the opening of *The Great Zeigfield*. They played that marvelous big organ before the movie started.

I loved hearing you tell me family stories. You had the greatest whistle I'd ever heard, but you kept it so silent. You always had the most gorgeous flower arrangements in the house any time of the year. And once in a while, we could get you to play "The Irish Washerwoman" on the harmonica. Where in the world did an aloof woman like you learn to do that?

I hated the drinking though, and was finally able to deal with it—and you. Of course the only way I could tell you about my feelings was to write you a letter. It all left some scars.

I still cling to certain things that belonged to you. I can't throw them away—three gray hairpins, your fur scarf, the plastic case where you kept your nail polish, and your recipe, in your own handwriting, for water-melon pickles.

I never knew what my place really was in your heart, but I somehow know you loved me.

The most important thing I've learned from being your daughter is to be very careful and vigilant about my relationships with my own children. I don't want them to doubt or wonder how I feel about them. Each one is special. Each one is unique. Each one is part of me and completes me.

I am so glad I have lived long enough to appreciate you and your part in my life. Telling you in person would have embarrassed us both, because what was yours was yours, and what was mine was mine. We never shared the two.

Profile: Sally Flood

Sally Flood comes to our interview dressed in blue jeans and a fleece vest. She looks very fit and athletic. She has short gray hair and a forthright manner. I am really surprised to learn that, at the time we meet, she is 75 years old.

Tell me about your work and your family.

I live with my widowed daughter and my teenage grandson. I'm divorced, for the second time.

I'm a retired high school history and English teacher. I worked as a teacher for 18 years, and now I've been retired for 12 years.

When I got married the first time, I was only 20 and had done about a year and a half of college. My husband was a sales rep for an oil company. We lived in Sacramento. I stayed home with my three children.

Then when my kids were about 13, 12, and 10, I realized that our family budget could not send them to college. So I went back to school. I was 32. I had the idea that I was going to be a teacher.

My husband's job transferred us to Seattle. I finished up my college degree at age 40.

I saw we couldn't do it. We couldn't stay married. All the kids were in school and out of the house.

We got divorced after 27 years of marriage. When we got married, we didn't discuss politics or religion on purpose—we were on different wavelengths.

I went through a big change. It wasn't hard, and it was filled with a *joie de vivre*.

I had an affair, remarried, and got divorced again. I've been single for the last 20 years.

Why did you decide to write a **Dear Mom** *letter?*

The older I get, the more I see my mother for exactly who she was, without any reservations. I am grateful for the things she taught me, and the laughs we had. I appreciate her for who she was. It's a great relief and release.

Were there any surprises for you when you were writing your **Dear Mom** *letter?*

No.

How would you describe yourself now?

I am an awfully good grandma. *(She laughs.)* Times three.

I am a good mother. I pay particular attention to the kind of mom I am to my adult children.

Anything else?

I like to read. I like to go to the movies. I've become more sedentary than a few years ago, but I still go to exercise classes three times a week.

When you first retire, you think you have to keep going. I tried a lot of volunteer work. Then I began to treasure my own time, so I made fewer commitments.

Has your mother influenced you in the way you are a mother?

Absolutely.

Because I never wanted the same relationship with my children as I had with my mom. It didn't bother me that they saw me with my warts. As they grew older I enjoyed them very much and preferred their company to that of other people.

My mother had a shell—and you didn't get beyond that. I didn't, anyway. Nobody called her Grandma. Everybody called her by her first name. There was something about the role of being a grandmother that was very uncomfortable for her. It think it came from her own mother. Her sisters and brother competed for their mother's attention.

I was one of five children. My parents' first baby died at 18 months, and my mother never talked about it.

So was your mother a stiff-upper-lip lady?

No doubt about it. She kept all of us vying for her good graces.

What do you consider to be your biggest successes and accomplishments?

Being a mother and grandma. Going to New York City. *(She laughs.)* My second marriage was a disaster, a fiasco. And I ran away. I packed my bag and went to New York City for six months. Then I found a lump in my breast and came home. The lump was benign, but I still had to deal with the fiasco.

Your biggest disappointments or regrets?

For a long time, it was that I didn't finish at Stephens College in Missouri. It was during World War II, and it was hard to get home. I wish I had done it.

Any other regrets?

I regret that my marriage to my kids' dad ended so sleazily. Not that it ended—but *how* it ended.

I could never be who I am today if I'd stayed married to him.

Stephanie

examines the stark contradictions between what her mother said and did about balancing work with family. At the same time, Stephanie tries to reconcile her own ideals and actions.

• • •

Dear Mom,

We sat and talked about those days when you went to work and I went to school. This was new for us; we had never really talked. As I was growing up, you were at work—with no time to talk.

That April afternoon sitting on your couch, we looked over your two family photo albums. In one picture, I was wearing a blue plaid dress and saddle shoes with white lace-topped socks. I had dark brown hair and a toothless smile. We had made pigtails, one on each side, with pretty blue bows. It was my first day of school.

You spoke of your trauma at sending me off to kindergarten as you started a secretarial job at the insurance company downtown. You told me how difficult it was to not be home when I came back from school. All you ever wanted to be was a mom, who would be home for her children. However, you had some bills that needed to be paid. Extra expenses that Dad's paycheck wouldn't cover. You *had* to go to work.

Mom, I never understood—if you were unhappy and only wanted to pay some bills, why did you work the *entire* time I was growing up? You knew it was lonely coming home to no mom, because you had grown up with no mother at home. Your divorced mother had to work to support her family. But at least you had your grandparents living with you. In the 1950s, I didn't come home from kindergarten to grandparents. I went to a neighbor's home down the street.

You told me how difficult it was for you those first few weeks of my kindergarten year, because I misbehaved at the neighbor's house. Our neighbor had some younger children. I remembered pulling the chair out from under the little girl as she sat down. Her mother was angry with me. As we gazed at the picture, you told me that after the chair incident, this woman no longer wanted to take me in. You were desperate.

I really didn't like the neighbor—or her little girl. I couldn't play or do anything, I had to just sit there and be good. But I never told you I was unhappy those first months of kindergarten.

We sat together turning photo album pages to 1954. I was in third grade and no longer wanting or needing a babysitter. By this time, my older sister, Cindy, was in junior high school, and didn't want to have anything to do with me. After school sometimes she called me names and hit me. I always wanted to tell you, Mom, how hard it was.

As time passed, I adjusted to your working. I started going to the park and participating in the after-school activities. I braided key chains and made pottery. I dressed like a boy and played baseball and football. I became an independent young girl. But as I grew older your words echoed in my mind, "The only thing a young woman should do is be home for her children."

I grew up in an age when all my peers were striving to be independent from the solo role of caregiver for their families. In your generation, homemaking was a valued profession, but yet you never stayed home. I have spent a lot of time struggling for a balance between what you said and what you did. I didn't tell you this as we sat together.

We looked at the photo of me in the fifth grade, dressed in a gypsy costume for Halloween. You recalled another day that year. There was an earthquake. My school was evacuated. The roads were jammed. You said how helpless you felt trapped downtown, a good 30 minute drive from my school, not knowing if I was safe. The phone service was out; you were unable to call the school or to come pick me up.

I remember how frightened I was, and how deserted I felt. All the parents came to get their children—and I was left. Finally, the mother of one of the other girls agreed to take me to her home until you could come. You told me you knew I was frightened because I didn't sleep for weeks, and you blamed yourself for not having been there for me.

A year earlier, when Cindy, my now 15-year-old sister, came back from summer camp with polio, you blamed yourself for that too. As we turned the pages of the photo album, you said, "If I hadn't been working, then Cindy wouldn't have been at camp." I patted your hand and told you that I did not think your working caused her to have polio, but you didn't hear me.

I never told you, but because you weren't home, you gave me the gifts of responsibility and independence. You also taught me to be a caregiver. Like the time I cooked a pot roast in the pressure cooker. I remember so much wanting to please and to help. You had given me directions: I was not to lift the lid after the roast started. But I couldn't see into the pot. So I lifted the lid—just a little. You came home and found me standing in the kitchen staring at the dinner, complete with meat, carrots and potatoes, all stuck to the ceiling! You felt it was a miracle I wasn't hurt and you felt awful that a 10-year-old child was making dinner.

There was my picture in ninth grade. You said I looked old for my age. When I got home from school, I would call you on the pink Princess phone in my bedroom to let you know I was safe. You had an important job in the claims department of the insurance company, and not a lot of time to talk. But I also called because I wanted to talk with you when there was a boy or a dating crisis. Or discuss the difficulties of being one of only three girls in the honors science classes. You didn't understand why I was taking tough classes anyway. That was something only Dad could help me with.

You and Dad had never gone to college. It was hard for you to relate to something you had never done. You could not understand why I wanted anything more than being a homemaker and raising a family. I could sew and cook. I liked to garden. But I had already done all that; it was no longer challenging for me.

What I never told you was how much I needed you as I started college. There weren't many pictures in your album of my college years, but you showed me a box with all my college letters.

When I went off to college, you bought me a blue velvet dog called Tearful Earful. He had a pocket in his ear. I could write out my problems and put them in his ear. The blue velvet dog would replace you. It would listen to my problems. I still have the blue velvet dog packed away in a trunk.

But Mom, it never really replaced talking to you.

As soon as I graduated from college, you no longer knew who I was. You couldn't relate to the new me, the independent young woman who was enrolled to be a teacher and was about to be married.

The pictures in your photo album show me smiling at my high school prom and at my graduations from high school and college. Then there is a gap. Eight years later you have pictures of my first son and me. You have many pictures of me raising my sons. I played ball with them and laughed with them over games. The holiday family gatherings are all captured in the photos. I could hear your words, Mom: "The only thing a young woman should do, is be home for her children." I volunteered and worked only part-time while my sons were growing up.

You worried that I wasn't strict enough, and you wondered at my unhappiness because most everyone I knew didn't stay home with their children. I loved teaching, but I gave that up when I started my family. I never told you how lonely I felt at home. I don't regret my decision, but it wasn't always easy to be home for my children.

As the boys entered school, I volunteered in their classrooms. You had never done that, because you were at work. We never discussed my passion for public education, my hunger to use my teacher training, and the need I saw to educate *all* the children.

There is no picture of me as an elected public official in the photo album. When I ran for the City Council, you told me how shocked you were that I was calling and asking people for money: I was "begging." Mom, it was difficult to ask for money, but you never understood that it was essential for me to do that. It was hard to get elected; I was running against an incumbent. But I won!

I invited you and Dad to be witnesses as I was sworn in, but unfortunately the event was the same night when I would vote on sponsoring abortion services in neighborhood clinics. You had already told me that if I voted in favor of the services, I would be encouraging young people to have sex before marriage. At the ceremony, Dad told me that you would not be coming. Later, he said that you had watched the television coverage of anti-abortion demonstrators. These emotional men and women yelled that I was going to go to hell if I voted in favor of the services. You never said another word to me about this.

We opened your second photo album. We looked at pictures of you growing up, your dog, your grandparents, your friends, and your boyfriends. You were laughing, playing tennis, or having fun at the beach. Sitting there together, you told me, for the first time, that your mother had refused to let you go to your high school prom party. Your mother was very strict and religious; she didn't think it right for unchaperoned girls to spend the night together at a beach house to celebrate graduation. You told me how disappointed you were.

Later, as I was driving home, I realized there are no pictures of you as a student or as a young secretary. The only picture of you going off to work is one I took when I was 10. I still have it in an album filled with images of my childhood.

It was then, that night, that I understood why you didn't come to see me sworn in. I understood why my professional accomplishments were not significant enough to warrant a picture. You were raised with different experiences and different goals. Jobs and professions provided money to pay the bills and buy things for the family.

Today, I just want you to know that you raised me well from your desk at the insurance company. I followed your lessons. I am a good caregiver. And I try to look nice.

Unintentionally, Mom, you taught me independence and freedom. This has given me the courage to make choices that weren't always easy. I made decisions based on a wide variety of beliefs and experiences, because you weren't always there to tell me what to do.

It can be difficult to keep things in perspective, but your photo albums tell the story: the kindergartner's first day, the graduations, the family holidays, grandmothers, and grandchildren.

Our families *are* the most important part of our lives. I love you, Mom.

• • •

Profile: Stephanie

Stephanie meets me for lunch in a vegetarian restaurant near her home. She is slight and has a polite, somewhat reserved manner. We start talking about an upcoming election and it's clear that she knows the players and the issues. Then we launch into the interview.

Tell me about your work and your family.

I'm 54. I've been married 33 years, and I have two adult sons. Both have finished college and are working. My husband is an architect with a busy practice and a fair amount of travel.

All four of our parents are in their 80s, and now all are living close by. I have a lot of responsibilities, taking care of them.

After I finished college, I married. I had my sons when I was still pretty young. After they started school, I taught part-time. Sometimes I also worked in office jobs. I volunteered politically. Then I was recruited to run for the City Council. By then, I was pretty well known in political circles, and I had a lot of community support. My opponent held some particularly unpopular beliefs, and I won by a landslide.

Being on the City Council is a demanding job. You're always on call, responding to constituents. I'm not a very aggressive person, and I found political life extremely difficult. I'm a great person to pull together a team, to work in a collaborative and friendly way. I learned from my mother this whole idea of looking for possibilities, for ways to accomplish things. That's what I tried to do, with some success, on the Council.

Why did you decide to write a Dear Mom letter?

I knew I had something to say. I wanted the opportunity to write down what was in my heart and my head.

In a way, I see that my mother and I represent the struggle so many women have, the push-pull between work and being a mom. I believe in putting family first. I learned that from my mother.

Were there any surprises for you when you were writing your Dear Mom letter?

Yes. The surprise was the ending.

Writing the letter helped me organize my thoughts about my mother. She had given me a tremendous amount: independence, freedom, and learning how to be responsible. My mother gave me gifts that last a lifetime.

How would you describe yourself now?

I have grown into the role of a nurturer. *(She laughs.)* It is a positive thing to do. I used to think I wanted to be someone valuable and public, someone to make the world a better place. But there are a lot of things you can do in small ways that make the world better.

Has your mother influenced you in the way you are a mother?

My mother is very conservative and reserved. She was that way with her children. I wanted to be not as reserved. And I was more flexible than my mother, about things like structure and rules.

I read to my kids and spent a lot of time playing games with them, hugging them, and just being with them.

What do you consider to be your biggest successes and accomplishments?

I have two wonderful sons. I've been married 33 years.

I helped make a difference on the City Council.

Your biggest disappointments or regrets?
    That I haven't done more outside of my family. *(She smiles, and laughs at the apparent contradiction.)* I don't have a long list of places I've worked, or an impressive résumé.

Peggy Bird

tries to understand why her mother relegated her to second-class status—and in her efforts discovers some hidden answers.

• • •

Dear Mother,

In the two years since your death, I've written thousands of words *about* you. Perhaps it is time I wrote to you.

Do you remember my asking you to stop telling that story about my birth—the one you said was your favorite? I must have been almost 40 before I had the nerve to say anything. It was only a little thing, but important to me. I'd just always hated hearing that your first words, on seeing me after I was born, were: "Oh, no, not a girl. What will my poor father do? Even the dog in our family is a girl."

I didn't tell you why I wanted you to stop repeating the story, and you never asked.

But I never heard it again. I think you just stopped telling it when I was visiting. It was easier than having a conversation with me about it.

There was a lot we didn't talk about. Mostly because it took courage to bring up difficult subjects in our family. Maybe that's what my writing gives me—the chance at last to "talk" about difficult things I need to understand. When I write, no one tells me that we don't need to discuss it, that nice families don't talk about such things.

I learned about what nice families did and didn't do from hearing you say things like: "Don't (run, jump, yell, go barefoot). We're not some shanty Irish family. We're lace-curtain Irish." Ladies from nice families, you said, always wore hats and gloves. And they never perspired, let alone sweat.

But I didn't care. I was trying to be the boy I thought you wanted. As a little girl, I'd felt like the practice child—the one who would do until the boy came along. When he did, 13 months after I was born, Wayne was the one the family fussed over, the one all the adults thought marvelous. So I tried boy things. At 6, I beat up on the neighbor kids when they stole my brother's bike, and at 10, I dumped my dolls to be Dale Evans when they played cowboys.

It didn't work. You only said what a tomboy I was, in a tone I knew meant that "tomboy" wasn't what girls in nice families were.

By the time I was a teenager, I was angry at being relegated to second class for something over which I had no control. I could never tell you how much I hated that Wayne was always first. The first to pick the color of his bike, so I never had the red bike I wanted. The one who was asked first which station the car radio was set to. The one who got the first slice of pot roast at dinner. I hated that girls waited for second choice. And got what was left.

In my 20s, when I became interested in feminism, I thought you might figure out the connection, but I don't think you ever did. And I never said anything directly to you. Nice families don't talk about things like that, do they?

Yet, with all of the things we didn't talk about, some of my clearest memories are of the hurtful things we did say. I guess after all those childhood years of not talking about emotional subjects, when I got old enough to talk about important issues, we didn't know how to do it very well.

Two conversations, in particular, seem to bracket my adult relationship with you.

Remember the summers we spent at Aunt Marguerite's? I loved her house. Oak Haven was truly a sanctuary for me. I felt freer there to do what I wanted to do—to run and climb, to crab and fish, to row boats and read books.

The house sat on a crescent of land worn away in the middle by the lapping waters of the Chesapeake Bay. Every day we crabbed off the dock, and every night Aunt Marguerite cooked what we had caught. I can still smell the cooking crabs, an odor that vaguely reminded me at the time of my changing adolescent body with its new smells, its new discharges, and its new thoughts.

A sound remains in my head, too. The sound of crabs scrambling to get up the sides of the blue-and-white spatter-painted kettle, out of the boiling water. Their claws moved frantically, trying to grab onto the side of the slick pot. But they found only another crab—and no way out.

After dinner, everyone would sit on the screened-in porch with the lights out to keep the bugs at bay, eating homemade peach ice cream. On the porch, in the dark, lined up in chairs facing the cove, I could eavesdrop on adult conversation.

One evening, the summer I was 14 or 15, the back-porch conversation turned to what my brother and I would do after high school.

I had recently discovered a desire to go to college. My school guidance counselor, as well as my math teacher, had been encouraging about my chances. Even the Back-to-School edition of *Seventeen* magazine, with its clear connection between a new wardrobe and college work, encouraged me. I was beginning to see college as a real goal. All I had to do, I thought, was do well in school.

As I was very good at that, it looked like a snap.

Although I can't remember all the pieces of that conversation, I am as certain now of the gist of it—and the key details—as I was the day after. You were talking about your hope to send Wayne to college and the barrier his failing grades were to your plan. Then you said something about my wanting to be a nurse and your hope that I would go to the three-year hospital program where your sister had gone.

I recall saying into the darkening evening, "I've been thinking that I'd like to go to college. Maybe become a teacher."

There was a slight silence before you spoke. "Oh, Peggy, there's no money to send you to college."

"I know. But Miss Camlin says there are scholarships and things. She thinks I should look into it. My grades are good enough to get help."

"You don't need to go to college. Your husband will support you. But Wayne will have a wife and children to support."

"But if I'm good enough to go to college, why can't I go? If I can find scholarships, I mean."

"You'll go to a three-year nursing school so that if you need to help out your husband after you're married, you can always find a job."

Stung by the dismissal of my still-timid dream, I let the conversation continue around me, and I don't recall how it got from there to what happened next.

What we said next, however, is burned into my brain, more than four decades later.

You said, "Peggy, you'll get married and have children. You'll do what I did. You won't need college."

"Well," I responded, "maybe I will get married and have children. But I know one thing I won't ever do. I won't ever hurt my children by getting a divorce from their father and going home to live with my parents because I couldn't support myself."

Aunt Marguerite and Father (the stepfather I adored) looked from me to you. Waiting.

You said nothing.

Aunt Marguerite asked Father about my stepbrother, and the adult conversation went on. I sat in the dark, my cheeks burning, my tongue thick in my mouth.

Many years later, I asked you during a telephone conversation if you remembered it the same way. You brushed me off, saying that you couldn't recall any evening like that—and you doubted that I could, either.

By then, I'd finished nursing school, married, and moved 3,000 miles away. You never seemed pleased that I went back to school and got a bachelor's degree. In fact, the roses I got to congratulate me on my graduation were from Father alone.

What excited you was my husband. You adored him. Told me that if we ever separated, you wanted "custody" of him, not me. I think I asked if that was how you'd finally get the boy you wanted me to be. You just laughed. When my husband did leave me, I wondered if you had been serious.

About a year before you died, we had the second conversation, the other half of the parentheses around our adult relationship. This one I'm very clear about. This conversation is not only burned in my brain; it's written in my journal.

It was July. I'd gone to Washington, DC for a week, visiting my brand-new granddaughter, helping my daughter get herself acclimated to being a mom. I called you before I left the West Coast and told you I'd be able to get to Philadelphia for a day at most but would plan a longer visit with you in the fall.

On the phone, you'd been so excited that Meg had given birth to a girl. Now there were four Margarets—you, me, Meg, and Maggie. The fact that you were excited that you had a great granddaughter rather than a great grandson was the first surprise.

The visit provided more. First, you complained that I hadn't gotten to Philadelphia earlier. Then you griped that I wasn't staying long enough. As usual, you didn't like the way I had my hair cut. And I didn't make lunch to your liking. Nothing I did seemed to dislodge whatever was in your craw.

When you began to have drinks that evening, your anger bubbled over. You picked over my 14-year-old divorce and talked about how much you missed my first husband, the one you said you selected for me. When I protested that I had moved on with my life and was happier, in my new marriage, than I'd ever been, you said, "Well, I don't know about that. I do know that just because you got dumped for another woman, someone not so high and mighty, someone who didn't have such a high opinion of herself, doesn't mean I have to give up who I like. After all, I met him first and he kissed me, not you, at Meg's wedding."

I assured you that my ex-husband's current wife would probably understand his kissing you but might be less likely to understand why he would think of kissing me, wedding or not.

"It's certainly not my fault you couldn't keep him," you continued. "I did my best with you. But I understand why he left, I guess. You've always been too independent and big for your britches." You rattled the ice cubes in your glass at me, the signal that I was to replenish your drink.

I got up, walked across the living room and took the glass from your outstretched hand. I went into the kitchen and stood at the sink, taking a couple of deep breaths. Then I poured a shot of liquor into the glass.

"Don't put so much water in this time. That last drink you made was watery."

"Sorry, Mother," I said and poured in another shot of booze. After I added a splash of water, I returned to you and handed you the drink. You took it, sipped it, and said, "It's a little better, I guess."

Your roommate, Doris, had gotten up from her nap and had come into the living room. She asked, "What time do you have to get back to Washington, Peggy?"

I looked at the schedule and told her that I was going to take the 5 p.m. train, two hours earlier than I had told Meg I'd be leaving.

"Oh," she said, "I'd hoped you would be able to stay for dinner."

You interrupted Doris. "Go get my other slippers, Peggy. They're in the bedroom, in the closet."

I left to get the slippers, but heard Doris say, "Wait on me, too, Peggy," with a laugh.

You took it more seriously. "Damn right, 'Wait on me, Peggy.' She's my daughter."

With Doris in the room, there was no more talk about my ex-husband or my character flaws. I packed up my pictures of the new baby and headed off to the 30th Street Station in time to catch the 5 p.m. train. But I sat in the station for two hours, numb from our conversation, until the 7 p.m. train. There was more air in the train station than in your little apartment.

I cried through most of the train ride to Washington. Angry that you'd spoiled this special time for me. Hurt that you thought so badly of me. Worried that the words came from the alcohol you were increasingly fond of. Wondering how to broach any of those topics the next time we talked.

I should have known better than to worry. In my phone call to you from Washington, before I flew back to the West Coast, you acted as though we'd never had the conversation. I didn't bring it up, either. It was easier to do what I'd always done.

Why, I can hear you say, am I telling you any of this?

Maybe it's because of your high school report cards. After you died, I found them in the blanket box in your room. They were neatly bundled together with an old rubber band, stacked in order. I read through them. You'd gotten A's in history, English, literature, and French—the kinds of subjects you could have studied in college, if you'd gone. You had almost flunked your secretarial courses—the ones you'd have to use for the rest of your life as a secretary.

I started to wonder: Did you tell me that I didn't need, and shouldn't try, to go to college because someone told you the same thing? Did you want a boy, not a girl, because you knew that boys got to do things that girls didn't, and you didn't want to have a girl who was disappointed. Like you were?

Is that what determined the dynamics of our relationship?

Or was it that I didn't live my life the way you planned it out for me—the way you lived your life as your parents told you to live it?

What made it so hard for us to get along after I was an adult? If I'd been brave enough to tell you this before, the way I told you about not wanting to hear your story about my birth, would it have been better between us?

After you died, I thought I could figure out our relationship, like a puzzle, from the pieces you left behind. But there were no letters, no journals, no diary. Only your old report cards and boxes of pictures. I search your face in the old photos, trying to read what was inside your head. But I'm illiterate: You remain a mystery to me.

I am left with nothing but my writing, the only shot I have left at figuring out our relationship. I try to get it to make sense on paper, so it will make sense in my head, in my heart. Trying to see, to understand, to figure it out.

If I had told you this before, would you have helped?

• • •

PROFILE: Peggy Bird

Peggy Bird, 57 years old, comes across as a take-charge, confident, accomplished woman. It does not surprise me to learn she has run political campaigns, taught classes on women and politics, and worked as a lobbyist. For the last five years, she's been a full-time writer, producing articles, essays, and prizewinning fiction. Her work has been published in *The Christian Science Monitor, The Oregonian,* and *Georgetown* magazine.

Tell me about your work and your family.

I'm married (for the second time). I raised one daughter from my first marriage. She's an attorney, married, and she's given me a wonderful little granddaughter.

I first trained and worked as a registered nurse, but then I spent 10 years working in politics. I ran Vera Katz's (now the mayor of Portland) campaign for the state legislature. And I've worked as a legislative aide and lobbyist for various public-sector organizations and utilities.

I'm one of those people who reinvent themselves every 10 years. When I got to 50, I asked, "What do I want to do with the rest of my life?"

My husband said, "Go for it: Do what you want."

So, five years ago, I started writing full-time: memoirs, fiction, children's stories. I even wrote a murder mystery—and got really good rejections. *(She laughs.)*

Why did you decide to write a **Dear Mom** *letter?*

My mother died two years ago. In what turned out to be the last year of her life, I wrote a lot about her, trying to come to terms with this difficult relationship. I never did figure out a way to talk to my mother. I thought writing the letter would help me understand our relationship.

Were there any surprises for you when you were working on your **Dear Mom** *letter?*

Yes. I started with the idea that my mother thought boys were more important than girls. But my thoughts changed somewhat. After she died, I went through photos and a box of her stuff. She kept all her report cards: She was very proud of how well she did in school. So then I focused on who my mother could have been. In writing the letter I came to look at her in a whole different light.

How would you describe yourself now?

I'm a writer, happily married. I have three daughters (two from my husband's first marriage), two grandchildren, two nice sons-in-law. I am more content with who and what I am than I've *ever* been. I felt that way in my 40s, but this decade, I've *really* learned to *like* myself.

Has your mother influenced you in the way you are a mother?

Yes. Both in what I do and what I don't do.

As a child, I always knew she loved me. She was very physical—hugging, kissing. I did that with my daughter, and I still do that with little kids.

But I knew I wanted to raise a child who was able to take some risks. My mother was the kind of mother always warning, "Don't ride your bike in the street," and "Don't wade out in the ocean so far." I didn't learn to ride a bike till I was 12, and am still afraid of the water. My daughter learned to swim when she was 2 and had her first bike at 6. And with my daughter—and my two stepdaughters—I am a different kind of mother than my mother was for me.

It's interesting: My mother and Meg, my daughter, got along much better than my mother and I. Meg was her only grandchild, and she was very proud of her. And of her being a lawyer.

What do you consider to be your biggest accomplishments?

Raising my daughter, a neat kid. No, now she's now a neat woman!

Having a happy marriage—the second time around.

Being able to say I had done in my professional life most of what I wanted to do when I was a kid.

Your biggest disappointment or regret?

That my mother and I couldn't come to some adult accommodation. Our difficulties started when I was a teenager, but they continued for the rest of our lives together. It's something I've accepted. Finally.

Laura

wrestles with her need to like her mother—and to have her mother feel the same way about her.

• • •

Dear Mom,

There's probably not much in life that I want more than for us to be close. I'm over 50 years old, and I want you to like me, to approve of me, just as much as when I was a little girl in braids. I'm supposed to be beyond that now, and I've spent a fair amount of time and money loosening those ties and establishing my own character. To a considerable extent, I think I've succeeded. Now, what I really want is to *like* you.

If anyone were to ask, I'm sure you would say you *do* like me, that you're proud of me and what I've achieved—even envious of the life I lead. Maybe outsiders think we take good care of each other when we meet for lunch or go shopping. But there's an undercurrent of tension, disapproval, and defensiveness that keeps us at arm's length. I don't think it's something either of us wants, but I fear the pain of breaking it down is something we both fear too much to try.

When we're getting along, I don't want to break the pleasant spell. When there's conflict, I've learned all too well that any disagreement can balloon out of control and send us both into irrational orbit. I hyperventilate, my voice gets shrill and argumentative. I revert to the fourth-grade girl who keeps fighting and arguing—not only to make my point, but also to win your approval. Now I try to say nothing. I know that silence is loud with disapproval and isolation. I suppose that's what I'm aiming for.

Yet I feel dishonest and enabling as I let you blame everyone but yourself for hurts and conflicts in our family. I see no memory or accountability for the cruel, biting, blaming things you say when you are angry. I can't even come up with a concrete example to share with you, except to say you've mastered the art of fighting unfair, dragging out past transgressions, and knowing how to zing into our most vulnerable spots.

In turn, I'm sure I give you more blame than is your due. I know that all relationships feed off each other—that some of your anger comes from feeling shut out, and some of my defensiveness is misplaced. I'm far from perfect myself. Sometimes I ask for more than is fair from both of us.

On the brighter side, I hope I've learned from that. The pain inflicted by one abusive outburst (whether it's aimed at me or others in our little family) takes longer and longer to heal, and chips away at any hope of intimacy. It's a lesson I'm trying to remember in my own role as the mother of a teenager, soon to be a young adult. The negative words and outbursts are starting to cloud all my memories of our family life. When I look at pictures and scrapbooks and even high school essays, I realize that we had a good life—riding horses, spending vacations at the beach, having friends over, and caring deeply about each other. How sad that those fond memories are often overshadowed by hurt and hostile feelings dating back to outbursts over things that didn't really matter. I know I don't want my own husband and child to see me that way.

Do you know what I resent most? It didn't—and *doesn't*—have to be this way. I know now that it is possible to love someone you don't agree with. To love and worry, even when they make poor choices or different choices. You know what, Mom? It's even possible to get along with someone who doesn't share your political beliefs.

Have you noticed that lately I've become more daring? I've said things that confirm your suspicion that I don't share all your views. After 20 years, I'm tired of nodding and agreeing for fear of being kicked out of the house for not hating the people you hate—and there are a lot of them. It's part of my cautious, conscious effort for you to know who I am, because—we've come full circle here—I do still want a genuine relationship with you.

I know there are deeper truths I should raise. I would like to apologize for the hurt caused by lifestyle choices in my past. Maybe I'm making excuses, but I've always felt you cared more about those choices than you did about me and my well-being. It would feel good to come clean and talk about those things, about what we both felt and feared. And I'd like to hear you apologize for the hurtful things you've said. Do you even know how much your words can hurt?

No longer do I dream that you'll give me the nurturing and wisdom I think of as a mother's gift. I've learned to turn to other women, other role models, for those needs. Maybe that's inevitable and healthy.

Now I pray to give you the unconditional love I know you cannot give. And to learn from your example what I must do to have a healthy relationship with my own adult child, and a contented, productive old age when it comes. I know that I'm sowing the seeds right now, so I say (only half jokingly) that I'm practicing my smile lines.

The haunting question, of course, is, "Am I fated to become my mother?" Do you ever think about how bitter and disagreeable your mother became? Does it ever haunt you? Is mental illness in our genes? Can I will myself to be grateful, optimistic, and generous as I grow older?

I know we are much alike in many ways. I have your intensity and your ability to turn problems into catastrophes and troublesome people into villains. So far, I have worked hard to learn from watching your experiences: holding onto my work, trying not to become overly dependent on my husband or too controlling of my child. Sometimes I fear I've leaned too far, asked too little. But then I see that a little of our intensity can go a long way.

It's not fair to you or me to measure my life and emotions by yours. You had different, far less loving, experiences as a child, and you came of age in a time and way that never gave your emotional energy a healthy place to go. There certainly are things I understand better now that I've walked the road of motherhood myself. What I would like to know is, did our road have to be so hard? Does it still have to be so difficult?

A wise woman told me once that all I can do in our relationship is "be the daughter." I can't fix your marriage or your insecurities or your health. Or even be your friend. I can only keep trying to love and to learn. In whatever time we have left, I continue to hope. *At least I can learn.*

• • •

PROFILE: Laura

I meet Laura at a popular café in her suburban neighborhood. She has a composed, calm manner and sometimes doodles on a notepad as she answers my questions.

Tell me about your work and your family.

I'm a graphic artist. I worked full-time until my son was born, and then I took about three years off. Now I have an office in my home. My son will be in college soon. That's going to be a big adjustment for me. Empty nest! *(She laughs, but she's also clearly serious.)*

Why did you decide to write a **Dear Mom** *letter?*
Because you asked me.

Well, really because I don't think there is any relationship as intense as mother-daughter. And writing the letter was a way of coming to terms with a relationship that isn't what I wanted it to be. There were things I needed to say, but I don't think I will ever be able to say them directly to my mother.

Why?
Because I don't think we could make our way through the aftermath. There's not enough trust in our relationship.

Were there any surprises for you when you were writing your **Dear Mom** *letter?*
Only that it felt as harsh as it did. I kept looking for good things to say, but they all turned out sour. This past year, though, has been pretty peaceful.

How would you describe yourself now?
Pretty balanced. Very fortunate. I have a really good nuclear family and a strong Christian faith. Honest, positive relationships with my husband and my son.

And I get to do satisfying work that enriches my life but doesn't dominate it. I have time for other interests: I belong to a book group, I walk, and I have good friend-ships across many generational lines.

I'm at the point in my life where I feel that it's "Grow—or die." So I'm trying to be more conscious of who I am and what I'm doing. My new theory is that being grateful is the secret to happiness.

Has your mother influenced you in the way you are a mother?

Sometimes very negatively. Both my parents thought I spoiled my son, but now they acknowledge he turned out okay, in spite of me. *(She marks this irony with a smile.)* My mother did influence why I chose to be at home when my son was little. I grew up with that expectation.

What do you consider to be your biggest successes and accomplishments?

(She answers with no hesitation.) My son.

I don't mean that he's a trophy. But I've found it very rewarding, being his mom. Beyond that, I hope, leading a reasonably productive life with time for important relationships.

Your biggest disappointments or regrets?

I know I haven't lived out my potential professionally. I stepped off the fast track to be a mom; it's been my greatest satisfaction, but also my greatest loss. Would I change it? No. *(She shakes her head, quickly and firmly. This is not an answer she doubts.)*

Marcia

looks at a childhood lost to her mother's mental illness. At an early age, Marcia had to take responsibility for her four sisters.

• • •

Dear Mom,

It seems as though I go through this dilemma every year. Buying you a Mother's Day card should not be so difficult, but each time I try, all the emotions I have about our complicated relationship surface. I wonder if other daughters also search in vain for the right sentiments.

I can't choose the verses that are soft and flowery, because you are the mother who always recoils at touch. Even now, in your 80s, the few times I hug you, I can feel you tensing up. I wonder how you were able to carry five babies in your arms. I wonder how you got pregnant in the first place!

I can't choose those sentiments that thank you for constantly being supportive, because I don't feel that way. I still remember *borrowing* the money for my college applications from you and Dad. Until I paid you back, you charged me interest! Yes, Mom, I knew that you were trying to teach me to be on my own financially. But I wish that I had had your emotional support. I wish you had been able to encourage me as I went out on my own.

I can't give you a card that thanks you for being the world's best mom. I know that if I had been the mother, I would have done a much better job. I know this even though I was unable to have a child of my own, because, for much of my childhood, our roles as mother and daughter were reversed. Since Dad was on the road every week, from early Monday morning until Friday night, you didn't have him there to lean on, and I was your crutch. You were suffering from what I now know is manic-depressive illness, and you often locked yourself in the bedroom. So I was the one to take care of my four younger sisters. I remember this pattern started when I was about 10; having so much responsibility on my shoulders at that age was difficult for me. But I think I must have done a good job, because my sisters don't remember the tough times. Their perspective is so much different than mine. From what they tell me, they didn't experience your illness and your inability to parent as major obstacles in their childhoods. Maybe I can take some credit for that.

I often ponder about what it would have been like to have had a mother who thought I was smart, talented, and beautiful. A mother who put my precocious artwork up on the refrigerator and admired it. A mother who didn't make me have home permanents to turn my straight hair curly. A mother who applauded the many A's on my report card—instead of focusing on the one B. I think I would have grown to like myself much earlier in my life.

I now know that I am smart, talented, and beautiful, but that confidence came late—and without your help.

My sisters think that you always believed that about all of us, but were never able to say it. I am not so magnanimous. Perhaps you believed that if you reinforced us, if you supported us, you might diminish yourself and what little self-esteem you had.

I wish you could have realized that you were handsome and gifted, with a wonderful sense of style. When you were feeling well, you were a great housekeeper and entertained beautifully. I learned those things from you and am grateful.

I am proud to be the person I am today, and I know some of that is due to your influence. Being your daughter, I had to develop my own strength. Your lack of confidence in yourself forced me to believe in myself. I had to rely on the reinforcement of teachers, friends, and when I grew up, the men in my life. Your inability to show affection led me to appreciate human contact, both verbal and physical.

I listen to others instead of talking over them, which you did—and still do. I still wonder what insecurity makes you unable to hear what I have to say. And why you are not interested in what I'm doing, in who I am.

Mom, I know you did the best job you could at the time. I hope you know that, despite the rocky road we have traveled, I will always love you.

I'm sorry that a Mother's Day card can't say that.

PROFILE: Marcia

Marcia is a striking woman, beautifully dressed and very pulled together. She's an energetic, ambitious business-woman who also serves on several boards, both social and charitable.

We meet at her downtown office. Marcia is focused and intent as we conduct the interview.

Tell me about your work and your family.

I'm going to be 50 years old next spring. I've been married 20 years. My husband and I were unable to have children, so we channeled our affection for kids into charities that benefit their needs.

It was tough growing up. I had to be responsible beyond my years. Basically my father, because of his job, was only home on weekends.

I *always* knew I wanted to work, to do something with art and creativity. I selected a college with a great program in interior design, and I received a scholarship. Plus, it was far away from home. Which I wanted.

I put myself through school. I lived in a dorm, and went to that school for a year. To make money, I worked part-time, designing retail windows. But it was the late 1960s and early 1970s; there was lots of unrest. I was paying a lot of money in tuition, my expenses were considerable, and yet classes kept getting canceled. I thought, Screw this! And so I did some research to find out where I could transfer and get credit and be at a less political school, where I would be able to go to class. I transferred to a state school where the tuition was much more affordable.

While I was there, I worked in retail and also did design work for a magazine. After I graduated in 1971, I became a staff artist at the magazine. I had good people skills, so in the summer I was selling display ads. I liked it, and I got transferred to that job.

I married right after college. I put my husband through graduate school. It was a young marriage, and it just didn't work out. We were married three years, and then we got divorced.

Then, one of my clients started an ad agency. I was only 26, but he asked me to run the agency. We did retail, radio, television, and newspaper ads. I did that for five years, and I liked it.

I was 29 when I met Jeff, the man who is now my husband. I actually met him at a business conference. We got married just four months after meeting, but I knew it was right: Jeff and I saw the world the same way.

I've done a lot of things professionally: I developed and owned a retail chain of specialty stores for 12 years. I've worked as a graphic designer and an interior designer. I've been a management consultant. And now I just opened my own home accessories store.

Why did you decide to write a* Dear Mom *letter?
(A noticeable pause.) It was nice to vent.

It was hard for me to write that letter. I put down

some thoughts I hadn't really faced. I know now that my mother did the best job she could, given her medical affliction. But I feel like I missed a lot. I missed having a real childhood.

Were there any surprises for you when you were writing your Dear Mom letter?

Maybe. I was really struck that my sisters had entirely different perceptions of their childhoods than I did of mine. It was as though we grew up in completely different households, which, in a way, we did.

How would you describe yourself now?

On the positive side: I'm a serial entrepreneur. Creative. Happily married. Well-adjusted. A good friend. Stylish. Athletic. Intelligent in a savvy way, not intellectual, but real-world savvy.

I am really blessed to have a great marriage and fabulous friends.

I have good social skills. I love to entertain. I'm a great networker, putting people together, making connections. I'm a good public speaker. I have great sales ability.

I'm creative, supportive, organized, and *very* detail oriented. So there's a bit of a push-pull between the detail orientation and the creativity.

The negatives: I have no mechanical ability. I might as well be a fish in that department!

I'm a relatively black-and-white personality. I do see more gray now than when I was younger. But still:

You're either my friend or you're not. No middle ground.

I'm exacting, meticulous, and compulsive, which is sometimes a negative. It drives my husband nuts. Also, I have a lot of determination, but I have to get clear on what I want. I don't like confusion, chaos, or disarray.

I feel really blessed, and I think you need to give back. It makes me feel good to help people less fortunate. If I can make one child think that she's worthy, then that can make a difference in how her life unfolds. That's why I do so much work with children's charities.

Has your mother influenced you in the fact you are not a mother?

I'm not a mother, but it wasn't by choice. For years, I didn't want to be a mother, but when I met Jeff, that all changed. For the first time, I had met a man who didn't need to be taken care of, so he could be an equal partner in childrearing. But unfortunately, we couldn't have children.

What do you consider to be your biggest successes and accomplishments?

My marriage is number one. The quality of women friends I have. My networking and sales skills—and my creativity. My athletic ability.

Your biggest disappointments or regrets?

The fact that in the last 10 years I have felt unfulfilled in my work choices. I'm hoping, with my new business, that that will change.

Ardene Byers Hogl

hopes that death will bring her the chance—at long last—to talk with her late mother about the many parts of life they never shared.

• • •

Dear Mommy/Anna Jane,

Somebody named Deborah Berger has asked me if I would like to write something—not too long!—to my mother. "Things I never told you."

There are lots of them—they seem to come easily to mind! Too easily, too plentifully.

One of the first or very early things I remember but don't think I ever talked to you about was your singing—to me and to yourself.

Songs: "Little Blackbird in a Tree."

"Little Bluebird in a Tree."

Children's songs.

"When He Cometh (white gospel)."

"One Sweetly Solemn Thought." I really liked this one!

Mommy, I have found a few of these in old songbooks. I pick them out by ear now, but I don't think I ever talked to you about them. I loved them all. I was pleased and happy and hoped your singing would go on and on.

Along with the songs goes what you taught me—and later my two brothers (Don, three years younger, Vince,

six years younger)—what you believed about religion—
"Now I Lay Me"—later, the Lord's Prayer. And others.

There were some unhappy things:

You made me apologize to Mrs. Chittenden, a
neighbor, for saying something sassy to or about her.
You were strict, but it was fairly rare for you to reproach
me. Maybe that's why I remember this after all these
years.

I thought what I said was deserved. You thought it
was rude, and it was. I still remember how it felt, not
being able to get you to understand my feelings. I tried
to tell you, but you didn't listen. You didn't understand.
What Mrs. Chittenden thought was what mattered
to you.

One time, I called you a hypocrite. You were always
talking about being tactful, and I thought that was
hypocritical. You grabbed me and shook me.

There were times I felt very special: After my father
got a new job, we moved to the little house in the
country. It was just three rooms and an attic. I was 11, and
you gave me the only real bedroom. I don't think I ever
told you how wonderful that was. Maybe I didn't realize
then what a sacrifice you had made for me. In giving me
the only bedroom, you put me ahead of everyone else in
the family, including yourself.

In one of our rare talks, we discussed pregnancy and
childbirth. I remember saying that when I had a baby I
wanted you to be with me. (I never had one.) I am glad
that I told you that.

Of course, I left home when I was 17 to go to college (for one year) in Iowa. Then I went to work in the Kansas City area. I didn't know it then, but when I was 20 and returned to Oregon for a visit, it would be the last time I would see you.

You died on Christmas Eve, 1931. You were 58, and I was 22; you were in Oregon, and I was in Kansas City. You were ill only a little while—I hadn't known. I think you were just worn out. Dad and the boys had had the flu, and you got pneumonia after taking care of everyone.

Mother—Anna Jane—Mommy—we didn't talk—most things I didn't tell you.

(And I don't think you told me much either. We couldn't—could we?) In those days the idea of really communicating with parents as people was very rare. I remember so well, thinking that you wouldn't understand me, about how I felt, or what I meant.

Maybe in That Good Place where you are now—I do believe—and where I hope to be after awhile—I am 91 now—I hope I can tell you then, all those things we've never talked about.

• • •

Profile: Ardene Byers Hogl

I meet Ardene at the home of Claudia Hutchison, another *Dear Mom* contributor. Ardene has white hair, a nice smile, and a face that doesn't look like it has seen nine decades.

We sit at Claudia's kitchen table, with a view of the mountains, and talk. Ardene tells me she is a member of the Reorganized Church of Jesus Christ of Latter Day Saints, now known as the Community of Christ. "People ask me if I'm a Christian, and I say, "What's a Christian?"

Tell me about your work and your family.

I wasn't very close to my mother. She never told me she was proud of me. It was common in those days not to praise children. The idea was kids would get stuck up. I don't understand this attitude at all.

My mother was strict—not warm or affectionate. But she held our family together; my father didn't do that. My dad had lived at home with his family before he got married. He had some money saved up. So we lived on that and on what my parents made, but it was a struggle.

My mother was beautiful. She was more beautiful than I have ever been. She was 34 when she got married, she had been almost a mother to her own siblings.

I never heard my mother say a word about sex. But you have to remember, I was born in 1909, and she was born in 1873. A lot of people were like that then.

I was a stenographer and secretary on and off from when I was 17 until I was 67. I worked most of the time. Every so often, I thought I'd stay home, but I didn't like staying home. I was married to a good Catholic for 41 years. We had no children.

Why did you decide to write a **Dear Mom** *letter?*
Because Claudia told me about it. I try to do what my friends want. *(She smiles.)*

Any other reason?
Not particularly.

Were there any surprises for you when you were writing your **Dear Mom** *letter?*
I don't remember. I like writing pages. I still do the morning pages Julia Cameron talks about in her book *(The Artist's Way).*
I was a little surprised that I remembered the songs my mother used to sing. Writing the letter was like going down a time tunnel.

How would you describe yourself now?
I'm 91 years old.
I don't see well, I don't hear well, I don't walk well— but I'm still having fun.
I have a new piano pupil, just one. I played in church, so people asked me to give them lessons. The same month my husband died, I went with my nephew to Portland Community College. I enrolled in music classes for six years. I learned a lot about music theory.

Any other ways you would describe yourself now?
Tolerant. That's an elitist word in itself. More I would describe myself as a person who believes everyone is as

good as everyone else, whether he's Bill Gates, or the guy in the city dump.

Has your mother influenced you in the fact you are not a mother?

The reason I'm not a mother is because we were unable to have children. I would have liked to have had a baby. I like children.

What do you consider to be your biggest successes and accomplishments?

Good question. *(She smiles.)*

Playing the piano well. It sounds good with the congregation singing. Also, I was a skilled secretary at a lot of different places.

I was married to John for more than 41 years. I was almost 30 when we got married. My husband was a chemist for a small independent laboratory in Portland. They did almost everything. He's been gone 20 years this fall.

Your biggest disappointments or regrets?

I'm not sure I have any.

Maybe that I can't see so well. This is not going to get any better. When you're 91, just about everybody is a kid compared to you. I still live by myself, but I have someone who comes in to help me.

Dear Mom

**Writing
your own
Dear Mom
letter**

Writing Your Own Dear Mom Letter

• • •

How did you feel, reading these *Dear Mom* letters?

Did you laugh in recognition? Smile in appreciation? Shed some tears?

(I know that despite many readings as I worked on this book, I still can't get through several letters—Claudia Hutchison's and Pat Pierson's come immediately to mind—without tears welling up.)

Now, maybe you're thinking of writing your own *Dear Mom* letter.

Sometimes—no, make that often—it is daunting to get started. To sit with pen in hand, or fingers on the keyboard, and actually write down what you have carried so privately, so carefully in your heart and soul. Maybe, like many of us, you are not sure what you want to say, and it feels dangerous, prying open the tightly locked chest where you have kept those hidden feelings.

I know it was that way for me. And when I decided to invite women to participate in this project, I spent several weeks drafting, revising, and refining the letter I wanted to send to them.

Here (in modified form) are some of the guidelines I offered in that first letter:

I want this book to reflect the real-life messiness, joy, hurt, and healing that are all part of mother-daughter relationships. *Whatever your truths are.*

Some points you may want to consider:

• When you picture your mother, where is she, and where are you? How old are you? What are you doing?

• What did you never tell your mother?

• Why did you never have this conversation? Did you run out of time? Did you never find the words? Were you protecting her or others? (Maybe you did have this conversation, but your mother wasn't able to hear you.)

• Why do you now wish she would know this? (Some contributors have mothers who died, but the wish may be there regardless.)

• We carry our mothers inside of us—they cheer us on, they criticize, they wring their hands, they tell us to "Get on with it." *What does your mother do? What would you like her to do?*

• How has your experience as a daughter influenced you as a mother? Or in choosing *not* to be a mother?

Writing the letter is a process of discovery. Along the way, there can bumps, obstacles, fears, and barriers to writing. Some contributors got "stuck" as they worked on their letters. What can hold us back? Here's an excerpt of a follow-up letter I wrote, modified to address some concerns:

• We feel a great need to be fair, and this makes us hesitate. *Remember that you can revise to your heart's content.* And remember also that you don't have to share this letter with anyone.

• Your letter comes from your heart, your head, and your gut. The editor in your head can stifle communication, put a lid on your roiling feelings, throw a blanket over what you'd like to get out in the open. I asked my own internal editor, "What are you afraid I will say?" Her answer helped me release some truths.

• A feeling that this letter makes some kind of final statement. *No, it doesn't.* Each letter represents a *snapshot* of the truth, at the time it was written, at the place the writer was. The "truth" about our relationships can change—and often does. So it can be powerful to look at what we wrote at different stages. I suggest you keep those first, second, and third drafts. *Honor your journey as you honor this most primal connection, the one you have with your mother.*

Having said all that...
Very early on, I knew that I was dealing with material that was universally powerful. And the intense reactions

I got—even from strangers—reinforced that belief. I decided that I would only *invite* women to participate, but in no way would I pressure anyone.

Indeed, as it turned out, I learned that it was not unusual for a contributor to change her mind. Several women expressed great enthusiasm and yet found they could not write the letters. They did not owe me explanations, but they offered them anyway: It was not the right time; it was just too painful; it was somewhere they didn't want to go. My response: If this is not right for you—for whatever reason—please don't do it.

And that's the same message I would share with you. Whether or not you decide to write your own letter to your mother, best wishes on your *Dear Mom* journey.

• • •

If you want your letter considered for inclusion in a possible future book, be sure to provide your real name, address, telephone, and email, so I can contact you.

You can email your letter to:
letters@dearmomletters.com

You can also send it regular mail
(please do keep a copy):
Deborah Berger
P.O. Box 19827
Seattle, WA 98109

Thanks

• • •

There are many people whose support, encouragement, and expertise helped me give birth to *Dear Mom*.

Foremost, of course, I want to express my heartfelt appreciation for each and every contributor. I am enormously grateful for their willingness to explore the deep currents of the mother-daughter relationship. I also want to thank them for their considerable patience as we navigated the editing process.

I owe an additional debt of gratitude to everyone (contributors and others) who suggested a contact, considered writing a letter, or passed along a name. And special thanks to Claudia Hutchison for all her efforts.

During the three years I worked on this book, many friends and colleagues generously shared ideas, read the book proposal, and were helpful in a myriad of ways. With much appreciation: Lowen Clausen, Lorraine Howell, Lorraine Iannello, Sue Lockett John, Chris Longfelder, Lois Matheson, Rosemary Mayo, Ginny Nicarthy, Robert Spector, Michele Weldon, and Teresa Wippel.

Mark Jordan provided expert legal advice—and warm encouragement that went way beyond the law. Elizabeth Lyon's support gave me a shot in the arm just when I needed it.

Constance Bollen, a gifted book designer, provided much talent and a calming influence. Rebecca Hughes meticulously copyedited the manuscript and put up with me as we ironed out details. The pros at Trafford pulled it all together with respect for the manuscript and a reassuring dedication to detail.

Thanks also to the National Writers Union and in particular to William Minor for his advice.

I owe a special debt to my dear friend, Winnie Sperry, whose enthusiasm for *Dear Mom* never wavered. Molly Squibb offered valuable feedback and sensitive advice from the beginning. My warmest thanks to Toby Burton, Mareatha Counts, and Nina Finkelman for being there. Thanks also to all my friends at FareStart who, with their positive energy, helped me keep my priorities straight.

To everyone who shared stories, trusted me with their truths, and helped make this book better: I feel privileged to have had these conversations with you.

And last, but definitely not least: For my husband Rick and my son Ben, much gratitude and many hugs from all the way down deep in my soul.

ISBN 155212956-X

9 781552 129562